PROPHETIC WORD BANK

MAJOR DAUGHTER

© Major Daughter

Published and Printed in South Africa, 2017

ISBN: 978-0-620-61744-4

All Scripture quoted is from the King James Version of the Holy Bible unless otherwise stated.

PROPHETIC WORD BANK

www.majordaughterlive.com

E-mail: majorwnl@majordaughterlive.com

Facebook: Major Daughter Live

Twitter: @major_daughter

ACKNOWLEDGEMENTS

My precious friend Jesus, thanks a gazillion for your friendship and for the opportunity to witness to people in this manner.

To my boyfriend of many years, you are a rare gift to me and to the body of Christ. I will choose you again, and again and again.

I would like to acknowledge and give profuse thanks and appreciation to all the workers and partners of GraceWorld, in His service, with us day and night to send the sound code of the Holy Ghost to the nations of the world. May God, my Father and your Father, cause you to flourish like the cedars of Lebanon.

AUTHOR'S NOTE

I pray for you, that reading and feasting on this book voraciously will result in a major deliverance: healing, prosperity, salvation, joy, peace, success and abundance in everything that concerns you. You have the power to overcome the world and to overcome the fear of death. You have the power to overcome all evil through the precious blood of the Lamb.

MAJOR DAUGHTER

CONTENT

OPENING COMMENTS

The declarations and prayers are prescriptions. They are to be spoken out loud at least three times a day. If needs be, double or triple the dose. There are no harmful side effects.

Fasting will put wings on your declarations and prayers. All the declarations and prayers in this book should go with fasting. You should go for 72 hours straight fasting. If for some reason this is not possible, then go for at least a 24-hour fast. After that, continue taking the prayers and declarations without fasting, unless you are led otherwise.

These declarations and prayers can be taken anytime of the day as many times as possible. However, for best results, begin your declarations and prayers at the midnight hour. Pray each point loud, repeatedly, aggressively and with violence. Please do NOT disturb your neighbours.

No matter what your situation is, you must pray each point for at least five minutes. Do NOT just read them. Pray them repeatedly.

Before you start with any of the declarations and prayers, if you are not born-again, if you have not accepted the Lord Jesus Christ as your Lord and Saviour, please pray the prayer of salvation on the facing page.

Pray it and mean it with all your heart. If you are not born-again, this is a very good opportunity to accept Jesus Christ as your personal Lord and Saviour. It is only then that you can enjoy all of God's blessings and be enlisted as a citizen of heaven.

To receive more information on your new birth or if you would like to get in touch with us, please do so by contacting us:

majorwnl@majordaughterlive.com.

God bless you.

PRAYER FOR SALVATION

Oh Lord God in Heaven, I believe with all my heart in your Son, Jesus Christ. I believe that He died for me and was raised from the dead for my justification. Your Word says in Romans 10 vs. 9-10 "that if thou shall confess with thy mouth the Lord Jesus, and shall believe in thine heart that God hath raised him from the dead, thou shall be saved. For with the heart man believeth unto righteousness; and with the mouth confession is made unto salvation."

I believe with my heart and I confess with my mouth that Jesus is the Lord and Saviour of my life from this day forth. I receive remission of sins for my soul and I receive eternal life into my spirit.

Thank You for saving me. Thank You for making me your child.

I am born-again!

If you just said this prayer, you are now born-again.

Congratulations! Welcome to the family of God.

INTRODUCTION

Christianity is a great confession. But many Christians don't walk in the light of this reality. *Baker's Evangelical Dictionary* explains that confession is closely aligned with the concept of acknowledgment. We need to acknowledge who we are as members of Christ's church, as the children of God, and we do this through the power of our speech. There is the idea of acknowledging or confessing of faith (in God, Christ, or a particular doctrine), and the acknowledging or confessing of sins before God.

Prophetic Word Bank is aligned with the former, with confessing and professing our faith. Most people become victims of life's circumstances; they find themselves beaten and defeated because they have spoken the wrong words into their lives and find themselves arrested by those words. Prophetic Word Bank is where we learn through practical daily experience how the power of our words creates the world that is our birth right.

We learn to undo the damage we have caused to ourselves and God's world through our wrong use of words, and how to bring the Kingdom within ourselves and those around us by committing only to speech that raises us from the realm of the eternal dead and the dying into a place where we commune with the Holy Spirit and the angels.

Proverbs 6:1-2 "My son, if thou be surety for thy friend, if thou hast stricken thy hand with a stranger, thou art snared with the words of thy mouth; thou art taken with the words of thy mouth. We need to understand the power of the spoken word and what it carries. Words are containers. They carry life or death, they carry faith or fear, and they produce after their kind".

Psalms 119:89 "Forever, O LORD, Thy Word is settled in heaven"

Whenever words are spoken, they go forth to produce that which you have spoken, nothing else. If it is negative words you keep speaking, then you will have negative results, no doubt. If it is life-changing words you speak, you will have life-changing results.

The Bible says life and death are in the power of the tongue. You can use your tongue to build your life. You can use your tongue to change the circumstances of your life. Even better, you can destroy sickness or disease by using your tongue. You can come out of a situation by talking yourself out of the situation. It is called tongue work. You may be in prison right now or in a hospital or without a job. Brother and sister, I want to tell you that you can come out of that situation by just using your tongue.

Proverbs 18:21 "Death and life are in the power of the tongue: and they that love it shall eat the fruit thereof." It really matters what kind of words you speak or what you say, regardless of your situation. When you always speak fear-filled words, you will always be defeated, but faith-filled words will get you out of ANY situation. Words will either make you victorious or ruin your life.

First things first. You will need to get enough of the Word of God into your spirit. When the Word is in you, you will be able to pull it out whenever the need arises. The results will be evident in your life. You will speak the Word of God—not fear, not sickness, not failure, not defeat, not weakness, not lack. God's Word is what you need to build and change your life. You need to constantly digest the Word of God into your spirit. Suddenly, you will realise that you have overcome all things. After that, everything will become small to you.

Prophetic Word Bank will help you to do just that. You will be able to digest the Word. You will inject the Word into your spirit. You will load it into your spirit, and you will change the circumstances of your life. This book, together with the Word of God, carries power. It will anoint you and cause changes in your life. All you need to do is undertake the declarations daily and study the scriptures provided.

The Bible says you shall decree a thing and it shall be established unto you. So go ahead, speak and decree that it is established. Hallelujah. You can never be a victim of circumstances when you talk like this.

Now, I declare the Glory of God upon you. I declare the Glory of God upon your family, the Glory of God upon your business, the Glory of God upon your job, the Glory of God upon your ministry, yes, the glorious presence of God is coming upon everything that concerns you now, and here it is, *whooooooooooooosh!*

CHAPTER 1

Directions For Taking The Prophetic Declarations And Prayers

PROPHETIC CRY

"My son, attend to my words; incline thine ear unto my sayings. Let them not depart from thine eyes; keep them in the midst of thine heart. For they are life unto those that find them, and health to all their flesh."
Proverbs 4:20-22

Suppose you are sick. You go to the doctor and he gives you a prescription and says, "Take two capsules, three times a day, before meals." If you want to get better, you need to follow the doctor's orders. If you go home and put the medicine away in the cupboard and forget to take it, you will not get better. It is likely that you will get sicker. If you called the doctor and complained that you weren't getting better, he would ask, "Are you taking the medicine according to directions?" The same applies for God's Word in Prophetic Word Bank. It won't work just because you have it on a table by your bed. You've got to get it in you! For Prophetic Word Bank to work for you and produce results, you need to make war and be on the offensive.

"For we wrestle not against flesh and blood, but against principalities, against powers, against the rulers of the darkness of this world, against spiritual wickedness in high places."
Ephesians 6:12

GOD'S WORD IS MEDICINE TO OUR FLESH

Right from the fall of Satan, man has remained his enemy. He hates man with a passion and seeks to destroy him at every given opportunity (John 10:10). It is very common in our day to find believers who spend much of their time praying against perceived human enemies in their lives. This is an error borne out of their ignorance of the Scriptures and a major distraction. The scripture says, "We wrestle not against flesh and blood,"

He hates man with a passion and seeks to destroy him at every given opportunity (John 10:10)

meaning that the real adversary is not flesh and blood, and, therefore, it cannot be any man.

Someone may hate, dislike or despise you, but that does not make them your enemy. Your real adversary is the devil and his spiritual cohorts of "principalities,"

3

"powers," "rulers of the darkness of this world," and "spiritual wickedness in high places" (Ephesians 6:12). These are not flesh and blood. As a matter of fact, it is the influence of the devil that makes someone dislike you. The trick of the devil is to make people think fellow men are their adversaries, which diverts attention from the devil. The world we live in and the things that happen are controlled from the spiritual realm, and you need to be conscious of it.

Launch the offensive. Do not wait for the devil to attack you, your family or your business before you launch an attack. Always be on the offensive with your prayers. Even when it looks as though everything is going well with you, do not relent from fervent prayer. Make war in the time of peace, so that in the time of war, you will have peace.

There are two primary errors when it comes to spiritual warfare. One is over-emphasis and the other is under-emphasis. Some Christians blame every sin, conflict or mishap on demonic attacks. Others ignore the spiritual realm completely. The Bible tells us emphatically that our battle is against spiritual powers. The key to successful spiritual warfare is finding the balance and being on the offensive in faith. On some occasions,

Jesus cast out demons from people (Matthew 8:28-34; Mark 5:1-17) and, on other occasions, throughout Matthew, Mark and Luke, He healed the sick without any mention of demons.

The great truth is that no matter the hierarchy of the devil or any of his cohorts, they are under your feet (Ephesians 1:21-23). There is no demon hatched out of Hades that can ever defeat you. Therefore, fear not!

PROPHETIC DECLARATION 1

I live in joy, health, peace and experience victory today because I live by the Word! I release the forces of life in my spirit upon my body, academics, marriage, business and everything that has to do with me as I open my spirit and act on the Word, in the Name of Jesus. I have been fully covered and wrapped in Christ; therefore, sickness, disease, infirmity, fear, unbelief, and all such negativities cannot be found in me! Glory to God! I declare that the life that I live, I live by faith of the Son of God, who loved me and gave Himself for me. I am moving from glory to glory and from strength to strength, in the Name of Jesus. I have the life of

I open my spirit and act on the Word, in the Name of Jesus

Christ in me. Therefore, I live above sickness and disease. The life of Christ is continually manifested in and through me to everyone in my world, in Jesus' Name. My life is welded with Christ in God; totally immersed in Christ. No infirmity or any other agent of the devil can stay in my body, in the Name of Jesus. I declare that just like the cedars of Lebanon, I am deeply rooted in the Word; I am strong, healthy and continually making progress.

PROPHETIC DECLARATION 2

I am an embodiment of God's grace. My daily experience is that of the miraculous and God's infinite love, in the Name of Jesus. I know who I am. I am seated together with Christ, far above all principalities and powers, and far above every disease and calamity plaguing the world and its system. Everything that concerns me conforms to the superiority of God's infallible Word. My body and all in my world respond to the Word of God, which is the sword of the Spirit. I am an active participant in the divine experience. Divinity is at work in me; I have got the very life of God in me. I produce the

Everything that concerns me conforms to the superiority of God's infallible Word

righteousness of God, even in my body, in the Name of Jesus. I am from above. I am a citizen of Zion, the city of God; the land where sickness is a foreign experience. I do not live an ordinary life because I am born-again. Sickness, disease and death are under my feet because I am a product of God's Word! I refuse to be weak and sickly! I have received life to the full! I am filled with the fullness of God. Hallelujah!

7

PROPHETIC DECLARATION 3

I refuse to house any "messenger" from Satan, because my body is the living temple of the Holy Ghost. He is at home within me and His life is at work in me. I live each day full of divine energy and vigour, in Jesus' Name. Every day when I wake up, I am full of life and vitality! My mind is alert! My body is alert and full of strength, in the Name of Jesus. Sickness, disease and infirmity have no place in my body, for Jesus has borne my sicknesses and infirmities in His body on the cross. By His stripes I was healed, and I remain healed

My body is alert and full of strength, in the Name of Jesus

today! My mind is daily renewed by the Word of God, as I diligently apply my heart to meditate on God's truth. I walk by faith and not by sensory perception. My life is regulated and conducted upward and forward, because of my faith in God and in His Word, in Jesus' Name. Sin, sickness and death cannot have any dominion over me because I have been bought with a price—the precious blood of Christ.

PROPHETIC DECLARATION 4

The devil is defeated in my life, and the Name of Jesus is glorified in me! There is an environment of good that surrounds me, and that environment repels sickness, poverty and death. I am above only and not beneath; I am the head and not the tail. I am a child of the Word of God. The Word of God is medicine to my flesh; therefore, I live in divine health 24 hours every day, in the Name of Jesus. The Word has been sent for my healing and health in Christ, the Anointed One. Therefore, no sickness

The Word of God is medicine to my flesh; therefore, I live in divine health 24 hours every day

can successfully fasten itself to my body. I live in the rejuvenating power of the resurrected Christ. I am free from sicknesses and disease of any kind, for the life of God is in me. I know who I am! I'm not the sick trying to get healed. No! I am the healed living in divine health. Hallelujah!

PROPHETIC DECLARATION 5

I declare that my body responds to the Word of God, and not to sickness! There is a disease-destroying energy in my blood that devours bacteria, viruses, germs and all agents of sickness! I refuse sickness and disease; I refuse to accommodate infirmity in me, because Christ is my life. Eternal life cannot share the same living quarters with sickness! I refuse to live in the dark or function by the lesser light. Rather, I function in God's greater light concerning my health. Divine health is my portion; I live in strength and

I refuse to accommodate infirmity in me, because Christ is my life

vitality every day of my life, in Jesus' Name. Thank You for the divine life at work in me! I am impregnable to sickness or disease, because I'm a partaker of the divine nature. I am a new creation in Christ Jesus; old things are passed away and all things are become new. The old life of pain, sickness and misery is gone from me; now I have a new life of health, wealth, prosperity and life in Christ Jesus. I walk in the light – the true light which is God's Word. My gaze is fixed on the Lord and His eternal Word, which guards and guides me in life. I declare that as I live and walk in the light of God's Word, sickness, disease and infirmity have no place in my body, in Jesus' Name. Divine health is my birth right and I live in it today and forever, in Jesus' Name. Amen.

PROPHETIC DECLARATION 6

I am a master over Satan, because my spirit, soul, and body are now saturated with divinity. I am a product of God's Word, for my origin is the Word of God; therefore, my words and actions are backed by divine authority. Thank You, Father, for the power, in the Name of Jesus, and the authority I have to use that Name against the devil, sickness, disease and everything that hurts or binds. By the power of that Name, I declare that I am living the life of glory that You pre-arranged for me, in Jesus' Name. I have been catapulted into God's Kingdom of light and life, where only divinity and divine health reign.

I am a product of God's Word, for my origin is the Word of God; therefore, my words and actions are backed by divine authority

The Bible says concerning me in Colossians 3:4 that Christ is my life! Thus, I refuse to allow sickness, disease and infirmity in my body, or to accommodate poverty and failure in my life, in the Name of Jesus. I have been delivered from sin, sickness and death, and catapulted into God's realm of abundant life where I reign victoriously with Christ, every day, in Jesus' Name. I live in absolute victory over sickness, disease and poverty today and always, in Jesus' Name.

PROPHETIC DECLARATION 7

I declare that I live, rule and reign above all form of diseases, in the mighty Name of Jesus. My spirit is energised for victory as I meditate on the Word of God today. I am positioned for the Supernatural life; I walk in joy, peace, prosperity, health and victory today, in Jesus' Name. I rejoice because God has given me eternal life and granted me the power of attorney to live in, and by the Name of Jesus! I celebrate the life of health He's brought me into, in Jesus' Name. I live a healthy life in Christ today and always, in the Name of Jesus. It makes no difference what I feel or see; my victory is assured! I thank You

> *My spirit is energised for victory as I meditate on the Word of God today*

Father for making me a victor, in Jesus' Name. I have passed from death to life, from sin to righteousness, from sickness to health and from poverty to wealth. I am transfigured daily into the image of the Son of God through the Word of God and the ministry of the Spirit! His life and nature imparted into my spirit gives me the ability to live above sickness, disease, infirmity and sorrow, for as He is, so I am!

PROPHETIC DECLARATION 8

I have the life and nature of God in me; I have put on the new man, which is created in righteousness and true holiness. Therefore, I live above sin, sickness and failure, in the Name of Jesus. I have received the divine life into my spirit, and that life works in my spirit,

Therefore, I live above sin, sickness and failure, in the Name of Jesus

in my mind and in my physical body. My life has been fashioned and planned by God for good. I have been recreated unto divine health, I declare that I am the workmanship of God in Christ Jesus, created unto good works. I live each day of my life, full of life, and invigorated by the power of the Holy Ghost at work in me! No infection can stay in my body! No tumour can successfully grow in my body! I am divinely connected to an endless supply of health. It makes no difference how the sickness tries to get in, that Spirit burns up every trace of sickness! There is a disease-destroying force at work in my physical body. I declare that the presence of that same Spirit within me causes every disease, germ that tries to get in my body to die and to pass out of my system! My body is the temple of the Holy Ghost! I am His living tabernacle. Therefore,

MAJOR DAUGTER

no sickness and no infirmity can share these quarters with the Holy Ghost.

PROPHETIC DECLARATION 9

From the crown of my head to the soles of my feet, the Holy Ghost vitalises my mortal body! It is not possible for my blood to be infected, because that same Spirit causes divine vitalisation in my body! That same Spirit that raised Jesus Christ from the dead dwells in me. The life of my body is no longer of blood, but by the Spirit of God. It is well with my soul in the mighty Name of the

The life of my body is no longer of blood, but by the Spirit of God

Lord Jesus Christ. Health is mine, divine vitalisation is mine! I cannot be sick because I am just like Him, and He does not get sick! I was born again with the resurrection life in me! The same life with which Jesus lives today is the life which I have. I am a product of the resurrection of Jesus Christ. I refuse to be suppressed or oppressed by the forces of darkness, but rather I reign as a king over them!

PROPHETIC DECLARATION 10

I exercise my God-given kingly rule over demons of darkness, over sickness, and over death! I have received God's grace lavishly and His righteousness; therefore, I live as royalty in this life! The life that I have within me is zöe, the indestructible and imperishable life of God; the life which knows no failure, no defeat and no destruction! I confess the scripture which says, I have been crucified with Christ: nevertheless I live; yet not I, but Christ liveth in me: and the life which I now live in the flesh I live by the faith of the Son of God, who loved me, and gave Himself for me (Galatians 2:20).

I live by the faith of the Son of God, who loved me, and gave Himself for me (Galatians 2:20)

The enemy has nothing in me because my body belongs to God. I am complete in Christ, and I have been perfected through my union with Him. The Name of Jesus has been named upon me, and I declare that my body is protected from all evil, in the Name of Jesus. Jesus bore my infirmities on His own body. Therefore, I refuse to be brought down by sickness. In Christ Jesus, I live in divine health.

PROPHETIC DECLARATION 11

I will never walk in sickness or defeat. The glorious life is mine now and always, in the mighty Name of Jesus! Christ purchased a life of glory for me through His death and resurrection, and sickness has no place in that life. Sickness has no place in me. The body of Jesus was bruised and broken for me; therefore, I refuse to be broken by any infirmity or disease, in the Name of Jesus. I declare that I am strong and healthy. I refuse to be sick. My body is full of radiant health and vitality, in Jesus' Name. Healing is God's will for me. Therefore, I declare that healing is mine. Jesus bore my infirmities on His body, securing my healing forever. I reject sickness, infirmity, and all the works of darkness, in the Name of Jesus. God wants me well! I refuse to accommodate sickness or anything contrary in my body. The Lord Jesus paid in full for my health and well-being; therefore, I declare that I enjoy a life of perfect health and peace always. My path is illuminated to see and experience the glory of God in my health, in Jesus' Name. Amen.

The glorious life is mine now and always, in the mighty Name of Jesus

PROPHETIC DECLARATION 12

Christ lives in me; therefore, no sickness or infirmity can dwell in my body. Jesus bore my infirmities, that I may never bear any infirmity! I am not moved by what I see, feel or hear; I am only moved by the Word of God. I am living in health 24 hours a day, seven days a week! No weapon formed or fashioned against me shall prosper. There is life in my bones, tissues, muscles, tendons and ligaments; I am

> *I am not moved by what I see, feel or hear; I am only moved by the Word of God*

alive unto God. I declare that my faith is alive and producing health in my body; therefore, I refuse to entertain doubts in my heart, for I know my faith always works. I am the righteousness of God in Christ Jesus. I have in my spirit the incorruptible life of God. This new life is in every cell of my blood, every bone of my body, and in every fibre of my being; therefore, no sickness can stay in my body, in the Name of Jesus.

PROPHETIC DECLARATION 13

I am superior to Satan; therefore, he has no power over me! The Greater One lives in me; no sickness can reside in my body. My body is the temple of the Holy Ghost; therefore, it is void of any form of sickness, in the Name of Jesus. I declare that I am superior to Satan and all the cohorts of hell, because I have received the authority of Christ; therefore, I am a victor in this life! Divine health is mine, in the Name of Jesus. The anointing of God is upon me and His presence is evident in my life. I declare that I experience the miraculous in my body everyday by the power of God's Spirit, in the Name of Jesus. I declare that I am strong and healthy. Sickness has no place in me.

My body is the temple of the Holy Ghost; therefore, it is void of any form of sickness, in the Name of Jesus

PROPHETIC DECLARATION 14

The Word is growing mightily in me, prevailing and producing health in every part of my body. I refuse to be a victim; I continually live above sickness, disease and infirmity; for as He is, so am I in this world. My words are potent and full of life. I declare that divine health is my birth right; therefore, I function therein on a daily basis. Every part of my body responds to the Word of God, in the Name of Jesus. The Word is life to my body and health to my flesh. I have been translated from the kingdom of darkness to the

> *Every part of my body responds to the Word of God, in the Name of Jesus*

kingdom of light; diseases and infirmities are not a part of me. I was born to be a victor. I am the offspring of God, recreated in Christ Jesus. I do not get sick, for I belong to the God class; because as He is, so I am in this world. By His stripes I was healed. Yet, greater than being healed, I am a new creation and old things of the world are passed away. Lack, failure, diseases and death have all passed away. Hallelujah!

PROPHETIC DECLARATION 15

I am the offspring of divinity. I am not the person I used to be; I am a product of His resurrection! Christ's nature in me makes me insusceptible to defeat, failure or any form of ill health, for greater is He that is in me than he that is in the world. I am fortified by the Word

I am fortified by the Word of God and strengthened with might by the Holy Ghost

of God and strengthened with might by the Holy Ghost. I am more than a conqueror, through the power of God's Spirit at work in me. The Holy Spirit dwells in me, so I am adequately cared for, glory to God! I wax stronger by the day and manifest the glory of God in my body and everywhere I go. I declare that I am a new creation, born superior to Satan and all demons of darkness! As I put the Word of God to work today in my life, I am changed into the glory that I behold in the Word and I am filled with all the fullness of God. I am conscious of the life of Christ in me. Therefore, I live the supernatural life today, above sickness, disease, pain, death and the devil, in the Name of Jesus.

PROPHETIC DECLARATION 16

I am positioned and inspired by the Word to be a source of blessing, nourishment, edification, encouragement, healing, joy and inspiration to my world, in Jesus' Name. I have the Word of God dwelling in me richly, in all wisdom and spiritual understanding. Therefore, I

I have the Word of God dwelling in me richly, in all wisdom and spiritual understanding

rule and reign over the issues of life, in the Name of Jesus. I experience health, and abundance today and always because I live in the Word, by the Word, and through the Word! The Word has gained mastery over my spirit, soul and mind, giving me a formidable mindset, the mindset of the just. I am not ordinary; I refuse to accommodate any form of weakness in my body; in the Name of Jesus, I refuse arthritis, diabetes, HIV, cancer, tumours, paralysis, kidney failure, and heart and lung failure. I declare that I live, rule and reign above them all, in the mighty Name of Jesus.

PROPHETIC DECLARATION 17

I have the life of God in me; therefore, I am "uninfectable." The life of God in me destroys sickness, disease and infirmity in and around me, in Jesus' Name. My body is the temple of the Holy Ghost; every

"Death and life are in the power of the tongue: and they that love it shall eat the fruit of it."

fibre of my being from the crown of my head to the soles of my feet is vitalised by the Spirit of God. I am crucified with Christ,

nevertheless I live, yet not I but Christ lives in me because the life that I now live in my body; I live by the faith of the Son of God who loved me and gave Himself for me. The Bible says in Proverbs 18:21, "Death and life are in the power of the tongue: and they that love it shall eat the fruit of it." Therefore, I declare that I am enjoying life to the full, in the Name of Jesus. I am dominating the devil, sickness and disease! I have overcome the world and its systems, in the Name of Jesus. I have the life and nature of God in me; I have put on the new man, whom God created in righteousness and true holiness. I am the righteousness of God in Christ Jesus; I am dead to sin but alive unto God. My body parts are yielded to God as instruments of righteousness. Therefore, sin does not reign in my body, for the nature of sin has been supplanted with God's nature of righteousness.

PROPHETIC DECLARATION 18

Jesus Christ is my Lord and Saviour! When He died, I died; when He was buried, I was buried with Him; now that He is risen, I have been raised together with Him. I have the miracle-life of God in me. Therefore, I am an associate of the God-kind, and a part-taker of the divine nature, having been made free of the corrupting influences,

The Word of God says, And the inhabitant shall not say, I am sick

decadence and destruction in the world, in the Name of Jesus. I have dominion over sin, sickness and circumstances. I am superior to Satan, and I have overcome the world, in the Name of Jesus. The man that could be sick is dead; in me today is zöe–the supernatural life of God that makes me invincible and impregnable to sickness, disease and infirmity. The Word of God says, And the inhabitant shall not say, I am sick... Isaiah 33:24. I have divine health; therefore, I refuse to be sick. I refuse to acknowledge any sickness, hindrance or limitation. Rather, I move forward and make progress in and out of season, experiencing times of harvest and abundance of God's blessings all year round, in the Name of Jesus.

PROPHETIC DECLARATION 19

I don't wane with age; rather my strength is daily renewed like that of an eagle! I am in Zion, the city of our God; here I increasingly flourish like a tree planted by rivers of water, bearing fruit in and out of season. I am a wonder to my world. My path is as the shining light, which shines brighter and brighter unto the perfect day; thus, my health shines forth, brighter and brighter with every new day, in the mighty Name of Jesus. I do not get sick because I have the life and nature of God in me.

I do not get sick because I have the life and nature of God in me

Divinity is at work in me and all things are working together for my good. Praise the Lord! I am a new creation in Christ Jesus; therefore, I am superior to all forms of illnesses or diseases. I refuse to be sick! I am more than a conqueror. The health of God is in me. The Spirit who raised up Jesus from the dead dwells in me and He revitalises my mortal body. I am sound and strong.

CHAPTER 2

PROPHETIC PRAYERS FOR DIVINE HEALTH AND HEALING

"For verily I say unto you, that whosoever shall say unto this mountain, be thou removed and be thou cast into the sea; and shall not doubt in his heart, but believe that those things which he saith shall come to pass; he shall have whatsoever he saith."
Mark 11:23

The Scripture above is a vital tool in receiving answers to our prayers. Whenever you have prayed for something you desire, it is important that you do not allow doubt into your heart. If you ask some Christians, they will tell you that they do not harbour doubt when they pray. However, their words, facial expressions and actions tell otherwise.

Doubt can be voiced out loud or in our thoughts. Many times, doubt is innate conditioning we are not even aware of. Jesus emphasised the importance of not allowing doubt into one's heart. This is because the source of doubt, which is from Satan, gets its grip within you. It then mixes with your contemplations, even while you pray. For example, imagine that a Christian is afflicted with a certain ailment. He takes time to pray about it. A few hours later, a friend visits and enquires about the state of his health. His response is, "This sickness is killing me."

Rather than expressing faith, this statement depicts doubt. It shows that this person did not believe concerning his healing when he prayed. Do not be the kind of Christian who prays for the sake of "fulfilling all righteousness." When you pray, believe for the answers. This is an essential faith principle in prayer, especially the prayer of faith. There are different kinds of prayers. The prayer of faith is one of them. Unlike other kinds of prayer (thanksgiving, intercession, and petition) where repetitiveness is permissible, the rule of the prayer of faith is that you should believe that you receive when you pray.

Asking the Lord repeatedly for the same thing implies that doubt is within your heart. For each time you repeat yourself, you invalidate your previous request. This is akin to a farmer who plants a seed one day and uproots it the next day. He plants it again and uproots it the following day. Such a seed will never grow. He will never have a good harvest no matter how much he desires it.

When you pray, believe you have the answers to your prayers. You have been ordained to receive answers to your prayer

MAJOR DAUGTER

When you pray, believe you have the answers to your prayers. You have been ordained to receive answers to your prayer. There is nothing too small or big for the Lord to do on your behalf. God is able to do much more than you can ever think or imagine (Ephesians 3:20). Just like Abraham, keep giving glory to God after you have prayed concerning a matter. That way it will be difficult for your faith to falter.

PROPHETIC PRAYER 1

Dear Father, I worship You today for Your greatness and goodness in me that has made my life beautiful and impregnable to sickness and disease, in the Name of Jesus. I have the life of God in me. I live beyond the limits! Eternal life is working in every fibre of my being, and I am full of the Holy Ghost! I am full of the power of the Spirit to live beyond obstacles and barriers today! I thank You for Your Spirit that lives in me, who causes me to

I worship You today for Your greatness and goodness in me

triumph in all things and perfects all that concerns me. I am a particular treasure unto God, born anew with the supernatural life of glory, divine health, excellence and power in my spirit! In my words and actions today, I show forth the wonderful deeds, and display the virtues and perfections of my Heavenly Father, who has called me unto glory, honour and excellence. I walk in the reality of my healing, health, prosperity, and victory today by my faith in God's infallible Word, in the Name of Jesus!

PROPHETIC PRAYER 2

I permit in my body only those things that are consistent with God's Word for my life. I give no place to sickness, disease or infirmity in my body, in the Name of Jesus. I declare that my life is an undeniable reflection of God's glory and virtue. I daily bring to bear the will of the Father in my life and my environment,

I give no place to sickness, disease or infirmity in my body

demonstrating the calibre of the Spirit. I have come unto Mount Zion, the city of the living God. Blessed be God, for His Word is potent and life-giving. The light of the glorious gospel has shone in my heart, and this Word is at work in me, giving life to every part of my body. In the Name of Jesus, divine health is mine. I've got zoë, the divine life in every cell of my blood; therefore, I do not get sick. Sickness is not a part of my nature. I am not ordinary! I may look like the rest of the world, but the life in me is different! I am separated, sanctified, demarcated, and partitioned from the corrupting forces of the world, unto the glorious life that is in Zion!

PROPHETIC PRAYER 3

Heavenly Father, I thank You for the impact of Your Word in my spirit, causing me to function in divine health and wisdom to prosper in all that I do, in Jesus' Name. Thanks be unto God for His enormous and blessed gift of eternal life, which He has imparted to my spirit! I am conscious of the divine life of God that is in me; and I bless the Lord, who causes me to

Thanks be unto God for His enormous and blessed gift of eternal life

triumph in Christ always! Thank You because my spirit is sensitive and energised to hear Your Voice and receive divine counsel, signals and guidance from You today. Therefore, I walk worthy of Him, fully pleasing Him in all things! I am God's perfection of beauty. The fullness of God, with the totality of His power, dwells in me, and I am complete in Him. Lord, there is none like You! You alone are worthy of all praise and adoration. I worship You today, and focus my whole being on You to do Your will and walk worthy of You unto all pleasing, in Jesus' Name. I am sound, strong, and getting better and better by the day because the Word is working mightily in me, in the Name of Jesus.

PROPHETIC PRAYER 4

I declare that Your Word is my light and my life! It is nourishment for my spirit, food for my soul and health to my body, in the Name of Jesus, and I declare that its mighty power is at work in me as I meditate on it and observe what it says. Your Word to me is reality, and that is the basis by which I know I will never be sick or defeated! I am thankful to You for making me a new creation, thus qualifying me to be a partaker of Your glorious nature! I thank You for Your Word in my spirit today. It stirs faith and dispels sickness, fear and anxiety, in Jesus' Name. I thank You for the power of Your Word and its ability to impact my spirit, soul and even my physical body. I am living in strength, health and victory as I exercise faith in Your Word, in Jesus' Name. Your Word is life to me; it is the light by which I navigate my way in righteousness, victory and dominion. As I give myself to Your Word, I experience its prevailing and transforming power in my life today, in Jesus' Name. Blessed be Your Name forever for Your light that shines brightly in this dark world, bringing healing,

It stirs faith and dispels sickness, fear and anxiety, in Jesus' Name

deliverance, preservation, and strength to the oppressed and afflicted, in Jesus' Name.

GO DEEPER

Exodus 15:26, 23:25-26; Proverbs 4: 20-22, 17:22; Psalm 91:10, 16, 103:2-3; Isaiah 33:24, 53:4-5, 55:11; Matthew 8:16-17, 8:23, 9:35,17:11; 1 Peter 2:24; James 5:4; Galatians 3:13; Luke 11:10, 21:33; John 1:2, 6:38, 10:10, 15:11; 2 Chronicles 16:9; James 1:17; Acts 9:32-34; 10:37-38; Mark 1:29-30; Romans 8:11

CHAPTER 3

PROPHETIC DECLARATIONS FOR PROSPERITY, SUCCESS AND MONEY

MAJOR DAUGTER

"For ye know the grace of Our Lord Jesus Christ, that, though he was rich, yet for your sakes he became poor, that ye through his poverty might be rich."
2 Corinthians 8:9

No matter the situation or dilemma you find yourself in today, if you would just take advantage of the grace of our Lord Jesus Christ, you will come out of that situation triumphant.

The Lord Jesus came to make us rich, not poor. He came to take away the poverty. He does not want us living in poverty. His wealth is beyond human imagination. Brothers and sisters, we need to reject poverty at all costs because prosperity is our right in Christ. So we are not the poor trying to get rich, but the spiritually rich, claiming physical wealth by faith.

The grace, as read in the opening verse above, has ushered us into a life of prosperity and financial abundance. You can apply that same grace to your business and job. His grace has brought us wealth. The Bible says God gives us power to get wealth. Take advantage of His grace to live in financial abundance and success. Declare these prophetic words over your life, your business, your job, and watch your life soar.

You will also have a Mother of Testimonies that will strengthen the faith of others.

Matthew 4:4 "But He answered and said, 'It is written, Man shall not live by bread alone, but by every Word that proceedeth out of the Mouth of God.'" Here we learn that man shall not live by bread alone but by every Word that proceeds from the Mouth of God. That means we have to find out what God said concerning our money, prosperity and success. What is

Whatever situation He found Himself in, He always spoke the Word

the Word of God saying concerning the above? We need to learn from our Master Jesus. Whatever situation He found Himself in, He always spoke the Word. Jesus was never quiet. He spoke to the waves, he spoke to the tree, He commanded fish to produce money (Matthew 17: 24-27) There are many examples of Jesus' prophetic Word bringing about miracles, through the power of God. What are you still waiting for, child of God? Start speaking the Word of God and prophesy yourself about your money, business, job, etc. Start taking your declarations, prayers and your confessions daily without fail.

MAJOR DAUGTER

Remember, you can come out of any situation if you use your confessions. How can one talk like this and be broke?

PROPHETIC DECLARATION 1

I have what God says I have. I am who God says I am and I can do all He says I can do. Jesus has made my life beautiful. Every day of my life, I walk in the reality of God's Word in every area of my life. I walk in the reality of the new life of righteousness which I have received in Christ. My path is illuminated to see and experience the glory of God in my finances, in Jesus' Name. I recognise the truth of God's Word that is at work in me today. By virtue of the divine life of Christ in me, I declare that I am superior to Satan; nothing shall be impossible unto me, in the Name of Jesus. I recognise that I am a child of the King. My words are full of power and authority. I commit myself, always, to talk like a king and consistently declare who I am in Christ Jesus.

I recognise the truth of God's Word that is at work in me today

PROPHETIC DECLARATION 2

My mind is filled with thoughts of God; I refuse to think wrong thoughts. My mind is submitted to the Word of God and I have a sound mind. His Word gives me the right thoughts to think and, thus, the right words to speak. I am born for success, for happiness, for prosperity and for the glory of God! The life I live is not a continuation of the old, but I am, in truth, a new creation! I am the offspring of divinity. I am not the man I used to be;

My mind is submitted to the Word of God and I have a sound mind

I am a product of His resurrection! God's grace puts me over and above in life! Christ's nature in me makes me immune to defeat, failure or any form of misfortune, for greater is He that is in me than he that is in the world. I am forever grateful for the blood of Jesus that was shed; I have been purged of all unrighteousness, and I am ushered into a life of perpetual victory. Now I have the God-life in its fullness.

PROPHETIC DECLARATION 3

The life and nature of God in me makes me invincible and superhuman. I am a product of God's unfailing Word of success, progress, victory and excellence, in the Name of Jesus. I prosper in every area of my life, by the word of faith that proceeds out of my mouth today, in the Name of Jesus. I am a possessor of all things because I am the seed of Abraham. I am enjoying the full benefits of my salvation and I bring forth success, strength and prosperity through the words that I speak, in Jesus' Name. I declare that the grace to constantly make progress is at work in my life, and I reign in Christ Jesus always! My life is an unending stream of success, effectiveness, excellence,

I am a possessor of all things because I am the seed of Abraham

prosperity and productiveness, in the Name of Jesus. The good life is mine, strength is mine and prosperity is mine! I walk in the Light, as He is in the Light.

PROPHETIC DECLARATION 4

The words that I speak are spirit and life. They are operative, potent and effectual, charting the course of my life in the direction of God's divine purpose and destiny for me in peace, joy, fulfilment, success and prosperity. My life is for the

I am born of the Word and Spirit of the Lord. Therefore, my life is a life of the Word

glory of God! This is my set time to experience the unprecedented favour and manifold blessings of God in every area of my life, in the Name of Jesus. I am born of the Word and Spirit of the Lord. Therefore, my life is a life of the Word. The Word in me produces a tremendous harvest of results in my life today, in the Name of Jesus. All things are mine to enjoy. I refuse to settle for a lower life than what Christ has made available for me, in the Name of Jesus. As God's representative in this world, I decree peace and prosperity in every area of my life, in the Name of Jesus. I am an heir according to the promise, and joint-heir with Jesus. Therefore, I am blessed in the city, I am blessed in the field, in my going out and in my coming in! I am blessed to be a blessing! Hallelujah!

PROPHETIC DECLARATION 5

There are no accidents or mishaps in my path, for I walk in preordained pathways of blessings for me today and always, in Jesus' Name. I walk in God's perfect will for my life today through the power of God's Word and by the working of God's Spirit, in Jesus' Name. The lines are fallen unto me in pleasant places (Psalm 16:6) yea, I have a goodly heritage! My portion is the choice one! I do not need to struggle for any good thing in life, because God is my chosen and assigned portion. He has brought me to a good place and maintains my lot. My spirit is energised for victory as I meditate on the Word of God today. I am positioned for the supernatural life. I walk in prosperity today, in Jesus' Name.

> *I walk in God's perfect will for my life today through the power of God's Word and by the working of God's Spirit, in Jesus' Name*

PROPHETIC DECLARATION 6

I celebrate the life of progress and prosperity He has brought me into, in Jesus' Name. I live a prosperous life in Christ today and always, in the Name of Jesus. I will not be a beggar or a victim in this life, but I will live to praise the glory of the Name of Jesus. He saw what I could be, and He gave His life for me, therefore, I will be that man or woman He believed I would be! I have what God says I have; Jesus has made my life beautiful. Prosperity is mine! My life is an unending stream of success, effectiveness, excellence, prosperity and

He gave His life for me, therefore, I will be that man or woman He believed I would be

productiveness, in the Name of Jesus. I declare, that the grace to constantly make progress is at work in my life, and I reign in Christ Jesus always! I am a possessor of all things because I am the seed of Abraham. I am enjoying the full benefits of my salvation and I bring forth success and prosperity through the words that I speak, in Jesus' Name. I prosper in every area of my life, by the word of faith that proceeds out of my mouth today, in the Name of Jesus.

PROPHETIC DECLARATION 7

I am what God says I am! I am rich, influential and strong. My faith is the victory that overcomes the world! I walk in divine prosperity and progress now, in Jesus' Name. The wisdom of God functions in me in such a unique way, guiding me away from trouble! Durable riches and wealth are mine because I am the seed of Abraham. My life today is the expression and manifestation of God's Word, which has taken centre stage in my life! I live in prosperity! I am conscious of the life of Christ in me. Therefore, I live the supernatural life today, above poverty. I am born for success, for prosperity and for the glory of God! I recognise today and take hold of my prosperity, success and excellence, in Jesus' Name. I have the life of God in me; it is the superior life of glory and success. Thank You, Lord, for making it possible for me to receive this glorious and wondrous life into my spirit, thus making me superhuman. I am a product of God's unfailing Word of divine success, progress and excellence, in the Name of Jesus. Amen!

I walk in divine prosperity and progress now, in Jesus' Name

GO DEEPER

Deuteronomy 8:18; Joshua 1:8; James 1: 25; 2 Corinthians 9:6-10; 2 Corinthians 8:9; Philippians 4:19; 2 Peter 1: 1 -3; 3 John 1:2; 1 Timothy 6:17; 2 Corinthians 4:6; Isaiah 1:19

CHAPTER 4

PROPHETIC PRAYERS FOR PROSPERITY, SUCCESS AND MONEY

PROPHETIC PRAYER 1

Papa God, I'm thankful to You for making me a new creation, thus qualifying me to be a partaker of Your glorious nature! I am fortified by the Word of God and strengthened with might by the Holy Ghost. I am more than a conqueror, through the power of God's Spirit at work in me. I declare that I am a new creation, born superior to Satan and all demons of darkness! As I put

My life today is the expression and manifestation of God's Word, which has taken centre stage in my life

the Word of God to work today in my life, I am transformed into the glory that I behold in the Word. I am filled with all the fullness of God. Papa God, thank You for making my life pleasant and beautiful, and for giving me a great future. I am conscious of the life of Christ within me. I reject every thought of worry and anxiety for I know that my faith in the mighty power of the Holy Spirit, and in God's Word, love and grace towards me is my victory over the devil and all the powers of darkness, in the Name of Jesus. My life today is the expression and manifestation of God's Word, which has taken centre stage in my life! I live in prosperity, in the Name of Jesus. Thank You Lord, for

Your glory that is revealed in me today, as I live conscious of Your power and presence, as I impact my world with Your glory, grace and righteousness, in Jesus' Name.

PROPHETIC PRAYER 2

I thank You for bringing me into a place of rest, progress, peace and prosperity, in the Name of Jesus. The wisdom of God functions in me in a unique way, guiding me away from trouble! My faith is the victory that overcomes the world! I walk in prosperity and progress now, in Jesus' Name. Christ in me is the hope of my triumphant and glorious today, and my excellent and successful future, because in Him I live, move and have my being. My life is secure in Him who causes all things to work together for my good! Thank You for the opportunity to effect positive and lasting changes through prayer. Knowing that Your ears are ever attentive to my voice to answer my prayers, I remain steadfast. Therefore, I do not stagger in the face of contrary circumstances, but uphold my victory in Christ, in Jesus' Name. I am excited about my new life in Christ. I have passed from death to life, from sin to righteousness, and from poverty to wealth. Praise God!

> *My faith is the victory that overcomes the world! I walk in prosperity and progress now, in Jesus' Name*

PROPHETIC PRAYER 3

Father, I thank You for the joy of being filled with the Holy Spirit and divinely transported into higher realms of life, far removed from poverty, death, defeat, destruction and failure. The eyes of my understanding are enlightened. Therefore, I see the invisible and I am empowered to do the impossible, in Jesus' Name. I thank You for qualifying me by grace to partake of the inheritance of the saints in light.

I see the invisible and I am empowered to do the impossible, in Jesus' Name

The eyes of my understanding are enlightened to understand and feel all that You have made available to me in Christ Jesus' Name. Your life runs through my being. I am a member of His body, of His flesh and of His bones! I am alive in Christ, and alive unto God. My way is prosperous and it is well with me, in Jesus' Name. What an honour to know You delight in me specially! I am propelled by Your wisdom to walk in the paths of divine prosperity and peace that You have prepared for me today, in Jesus' Name.

PROPHETIC PRAYER 4

I thank You for giving me a life of continuous progress and prosperity through the Word, in the Name of Jesus. Thank You for making me a testimony and the inheritor of the blessings of Abraham through my association with Christ. I am prospering and living in the manifestation of Your infinite blessings because I am Abraham's seed. I refuse to lack any good thing, knowing that the Lord is my shepherd, and I have been blessed with all spiritual blessings in heavenly places in Christ Jesus. Thank You for the victorious life You have called me into—a triumphant life above

Thank You for the victorious life You have called me into— a triumphant life above poverty. I have been catapulted into God's Kingdom of light and life, where only divinity, success and prosperity reign

poverty. I have been catapulted into God's Kingdom of light and life, where only divinity, success and prosperity reign. I lay all burdens at Your feet and choose the stress-free life! Thank You for taking charge of my family, health, finances and all that concerns me. I live in absolute joy today, in Jesus' Name. Thank You for the infallibility of Your Word and its prevailing power in my life! My confidence and trust is in the ability of Your Word to build me up and make me all that You have destined me to be.

MAJOR DAUGTER

CHAPTER 5

PROPHETIC DECLARATIONS FOR PROBLEMATIC SITUATIONS

MAJOR DAUGTER

"That if thou shalt confess with thy mouth the Lord Jesus, and shalt believe in thine heart that God hath raised Him from the dead, thou shalt be saved. For with the heart man believeth unto righteousness; and with the mouth confession is made unto salvation."
Romans 10:9-10

"Can two walk together, except they be agreed?"
Amos 3:3

I would like us to look at the word *confess* on the opening scripture in the light of where it originates. Confess as used in the above scripture means "to speak the same thing in agreement with God." This word originates from the Greek word *homologia*, which means "speaking the same thing in agreement." That

> *If you learn to speak with your mouth the same things God has written concerning you in His Word, salvation, which ultimately refers to the good life, becomes yours*

means you would be saying the same things that God said. This is the same rule for salvation. This is not just talking about being saved from sin or from the evil one. It is about being saved from all negative forces and situations of life. The rule of confession is this; if you learn to speak with your mouth the same things God

60

has written concerning you in His Word, salvation, which ultimately refers to the good life, becomes yours. So what are you still waiting for? Come on; talk yourself out of that dilemma, whatever its name is.

PROPHETIC DECLARATION 1

My confessions of faith come to pass because my words are anointed to produce results. There is no hopeless situation I cannot change, for my faith is the victory that overcomes the world. The life of God is in me, from the crown of my head to the soles of my feet. I live the supernatural life of Christ in the natural realm.

The life of God is in me, from the crown of my head to the soles of my feet

Therefore, failure, defeat and death are alien to me, because I do not operate as a mere man. Praise the Lord, I know who I am! I have found my place. I have discovered the glorious life that Christ has given me; a life of success and victory 24 hours a day, seven days a week, 365 days a year. It is success and victory all the way and all my days! The presence of God with me makes the difference in me, and separates me from the problems of the world. The life of God within bubbles inside me, and puts a spring in my step every day! I know who I am! I am full of life! Jesus said, "I am come that they might have life, and that they might have it more abundantly" (John 10:10).

PROPHETIC DECLARATION 2

I have received the fullness of life! Victory is mine and strength is mine, in the Name of Jesus. My mind is renewed daily by the Word of God as I diligently apply my heart to meditate on God's truth. I walk by faith and not by sensory perception. My life is regulated and conducted upward and forward, because of my faith in God and in His Word, in Jesus' Name. I speak the wisdom of God in every situation that I face. I am not moved by the negative and corrupting influences of the world, but I am guided by the true light of God's Word. My mind is filled with the thoughts of God. I refuse to think wrong thoughts. I reject negative thoughts and I declare that my mind is submitted to the Word of God. That Word gives me the thoughts to think and, thus, words to speak. Hallelujah!

> *My mind is renewed daily by the Word of God as I diligently apply my heart to meditate on God's truth*

PROPHETIC DECLARATION 3

Blessed Father, by the power of Your Spirit, I am effecting changes in every situation or circumstance that is not consistent with Your Word concerning me, in the Name of Jesus. I thank You for Your Word and its ability to recreate my world. Today, I take advantage of Your Word and create joy, success, peace and victory in my life and those of my family members, in the Name of Jesus. I am confident of this very thing that the life of God is in me. Therefore, failure, defeat and death are not a part of my life because the life that is at work in me is superior to the devil and all his works. I thank You for the victorious life You have called me into; a triumphant life above defeat, failure, death and every form of mishap. I have been catapulted into God's Kingdom of light and life, where only divinity, success, victory, joy, and peace reign.

I am confident of this very thing that the life of God is in me

PROPHETIC DECLARATION 4

I recognise Your divine ability, efficiency and might that are at work in me today, and by virtue of the divine life of Christ in me, I declare that I am superior to Satan; nothing shall be impossible unto me, in the Name of Jesus. I live in the Name of Jesus; therefore, no weapon of darkness fashioned against me shall prosper! My spirit is energised for victory as I meditate on the Word of God today. I am positioned for the Supernatural life; I walk in joy, peace and victory today, in Jesus' Name. The lines are fallen unto me in pleasant places; yea, I have a goodly heritage! My portion is the choice one! I don't need to struggle for any good thing in life, because God is my chosen and assigned portion; He has brought me to a good place and maintains my lot. I rejoice because God has given me eternal life and granted me the power of attorney to live by the Name of Jesus!

My spirit is energised for victory as I meditate on the Word of God today

PROPHETIC DECLARATION 5

I celebrate the life of peace, glory, progress, success, and victory He has brought me into, in Jesus' Name. I live a happy, successful and victorious life in Christ today and always, in the Name of Jesus. I function in, and live by, the power of the Name of Jesus today. Miracles are wrought in my life, job, business, family and ministry, and circumstances conform to God's perfect will for me, in Jesus' Name. The Word of God in my mouth is my victory over adversities and the challenges of life! I am making progress, moving forward, and growing in grace, righteousness and the knowledge of the Lord; and there is no stopping me! My destiny is shaped in line with God's perfect will for me, in Jesus' Name. The anointing which I have received of the Lord, abides in me forever, and through that anointing I am energised for productivity and positioned for effectiveness! I take advantage of that anointing today, to bless my world and do exploits to the glory and praise of His Name. Amen.

I live a happy, successful and victorious life in Christ today and always

PROPHETIC DECLARATION 6

I am a faith-child of a faith-God! I live today in victory and triumph because I am fully persuaded that I am what God says I am, I have what He says I have, and I can do what He says I can do. The Word has gone forth concerning me that I am a champion in this life, and so it is! I live in dominion over the elements and principles of the world and its systems! I am born of God, I hail from God,

The Word has gone forth concerning me that I am a champion in this life, and so it is

my origin is in God, and therefore I overcome the world! How could I fail? It is impossible! I live by the faith of Jesus! Greater is He that is in me, than he that is in the world! I recognise the truth of God's Word that is at work in me today, and by virtue of the divine life of Christ in me, I declare that I am superior to Satan; nothing shall be impossible unto me, in the Name of Jesus. I recognise that I am a child of the King and my words are full of power and authority. I commit myself to always talk like a king, and consistently declare who I am in Christ Jesus. My mind is filled with the thoughts of God; I refuse to think wrong thoughts. My mind is submitted to the Word of God and I have a sound mind. His Word gives me the right thoughts to think and thus, the right words to speak. Victory is mine, strength is mine and peace is mine! For I walk in the light, as He is in the light.

PROPHETIC DECLARATION 7

Thank You, Lord Jesus, for giving me the right to reign and rule over the circumstances of life and exercise dominion over Satan and the power of darkness. I am seated together with Christ in heavenly realms, far above all principality and power! I exercise the authority of Christ in and around my sphere of contact, in Jesus' Name. The life and nature of God in me makes me invincible and superhuman. I am a product of God's unfailing Word of divine success, progress, victory and excellence, in the Name of Jesus. I am an ordained saint of God, with the life of God and His nature

I exercise the authority of Christ in and around my sphere of contact, in Jesus' Name

of righteousness. Therefore, I have right standing with God and reign over the challenges, problems and circumstances of this world, in the Name of Jesus. Precious Lord, thank You for justifying me and making me blameless in Your sight. I refuse to allow the devil or the opinions of others, or even my mind, to put me in a place of self-condemnation. I am free to serve You and free to live the good life, in the Name of Jesus.

PROPHETIC DECLARATION 8

No weapon of darkness fashioned against me shall prosper, because I live in the Name of Jesus! I have been delivered from sin, failure and death, and catapulted into God's realm of abundance where I reign victoriously with Christ, every day, in Jesus' Name. I am positioned in the centre of God's perfect will, taking the paths of glory which God prearranged for me to walk in as I consciously live in the light of God's Word today and always, in Jesus' Name.

Knowing that Your ears are ever attentive to my voice to answer my prayers, I remain steadfast

Thank You for the opportunity to effect positive and lasting changes through prayer. Knowing that Your ears are ever attentive to my voice to answer my prayers, I remain steadfast. Therefore, I do not stagger in the face of contrary circumstances, but uphold my victory in Christ, in Jesus' Name. Thank You for loving and caring for me affectionately. I give room for Your peace to mount guard over my heart. I reject anxiety, worry and stress. I choose to live in joy and rest today and every day, in the Name of Jesus.

PROPHETIC DECLARATION 9

I refuse to be troubled or worried by circumstances because with the Word of God in my mouth, I can change negative situations and create a suitable life of glory, victory and fulfilment, in Jesus' Name. I thank You for creating me for Your pleasure, making provisions for me to live a glorious and extraordinary life of victory from a position of rest! I function today with joy, knowing that my future is secure in You, in Jesus' Name. Your Word in my spirit is growing mightily, building my faith strong and gaining

Your Word in my spirit is growing mightily, building my faith strong and gaining supremacy in my life

supremacy in my life! I boldly resist and nullify every contrary work or opposition from the enemy today, standing my ground in the victory Christ obtained for me, in Jesus' Name. I lay all burdens at Your feet, and choose the stress-free life! Thank You for taking charge of my family and all that concerns me; I live in absolute joy today, in Jesus' Name.

GO DEEPER

Romans 8:28; James 1:2-4; 1 Peter 5:7; 2 Corinthians 4:17; Proverbs 24:10; 1 John 4:4; 1 Corinthians 10:13; Psalm 127:2; Ecclesiastes 8:4

CHAPTER 6

PROPHETIC PRAYERS FOR PROBLEMATIC SITUATIONS

PROPHETIC PRAYER 1

Father, thank You for loading me daily with all the benefits of life, such that I am thoroughly furnished with all I need to live joyfully today, in the Name of Jesus. I thank You that my faith in Your Word prevails no matter what I hear, see or feel. I walk in victory and dominion today, in Jesus' Name. I look at the world from the mountaintop! I see as God sees! I look with the eyes of faith. I am not subject to the elements of

I carry my own atmosphere everywhere I go; an atmosphere of divine peace

this world. I have overcome the world! I am not subject to the world. I carry my own atmosphere everywhere I go; an atmosphere of divine peace. I testify that I have overcome the world, sin and the devil because I am born of God. I have His very life in me and that makes me invincible and superhuman. I declare that in my life, all things are working together for my good because I love God, and I have been called according to His purpose. Every situation that I face is a stepping stone for me. In every area of my life, things are working out for my good; great peace and strength are my portion every day, in the Name of Jesus. Amen.

PROPHETIC PRAYER 2

Holy Father, thank You for giving me the Word of God; the material for cleansing and renewing my mind to be conformed to the image of Your Son. I refuse to set my mind on the things of this world, having put on the new man, which is recreated in righteousness and true holiness, in Jesus' Name.

Blessed be God, in whom I live, and move, and have my being. How I love and appreciate You today, righteous Father! I live for

How I love and appreciate You today, righteous Father! I live for You alone, and rejoice that I belong to You

You alone, and rejoice that I belong to You. I am fulfilled with all the pleasures of Your goodness, and the work of faith with power, in Jesus' Name. I live the supernatural life in Christ Jesus—a life beyond the ordinary level of perception and comprehension. I walk in victory, success, divine peace, abundance, excellence and glory, in the Name of Jesus.

PROPHETIC PRAYER 3

Father, I receive direction, inspiration, counsel, wisdom and enlightenment from Your Holy Spirit as I remain in fellowship with You today, through the Word and prayer. I am strengthened, energised and positioned for greater levels of glory and excellence in life, in Jesus' Name. I thank You for filling my heart with Your love. I am humbled by the greatness of Your love and the magnitude of Your grace towards me. I walk in the consciousness of Your great love for me today, in Jesus' Name. I thank You for Your Spirit that lives in me, who causes me to triumph in all things and perfects all that concerns me. My life is transformed, and my spirit is conditioned for success, dominion and victory as I meditate on the Word of God daily. I am strengthened and lifted by Your Word today, and my faith prevails against all opposing forces as I put Your Word to work and take possession of all that belongs to me in Christ Jesus. Amen.

I am humbled by the greatness of Your love and the magnitude of Your grace towards me

PROPHETIC PRAYER 4

Dear Father, my spirit is attuned to You and attentive to Your voice today. I look away from everything else and focus my gaze on Your Word. Your glory is revealed in me and I walk in the realities of Your Kingdom, in Jesus' Name. I do not acknowledge any condition that is not in line with the Word. I give no room to the ideologies of men; rather, I constantly inundate my mind with the Word, taking full hold of that which has been consummated by the suffering, death and resurrection of Jesus. My

My spiritual eyes are constantly open to see, my heart is fertile ground for the Word to flourish and prevail

spiritual eyes are constantly open to see, my heart is fertile ground for the Word to flourish and prevail. I am energised from within. I am walking in victory now and always. I prosper in all things in Jesus' mighty Name.

PROPHETIC PRAYER 5

I refuse to be limited by contrary forces and conditions around me; I accomplish the impossible, I do the spectacular and I reach for the peak in all my endeavours by the power of the Holy Spirit. God's Word is at work in me; my life is the mirror image of what the Word talks about. I am the light of my world and I shine everywhere I go, in the Name of Jesus. I continually fix my gaze on the Word of God. My

I reach for the peak in all my endeavours by the power of the Holy Spirit

thoughts, words and actions are inspired by faith in God's eternal Word and the leading of His Spirit. I am not moved by what I see, feel or hear, but I respond only in faith in the Word of God. Everything I require for life and godliness has been delivered unto me, and I am enjoying life to the full, in Jesus' Name. I declare that all things are working together for my good because I love the Lord, and I have been called according to His purpose. Amen.

PROPHETIC PRAYER 6

Dear Father, I thank You for Your Word and its ability to renew my mind and transform me from glory to glory. I lay hold of my miracle today, and take charge of circumstances as I activate the power of the Spirit by acting on the Word. I thank You today for giving me Your righteousness as a gift. I reign and rule as a king today, as I boldly take advantage of my right standing with You, in Jesus' Name. I experience increasing joy, happiness, peace and productivity as I absolve others of their

> *I thank You today for giving me Your righteousness as a gift. I reign and rule as a king today, as I boldly take advantage of my right standing with You, in Jesus' Name*

faults and demonstrate only love towards them, in the Name of Jesus. My faith in God's Word, amidst all opposing circumstances, is the victory that overcomes the world and every adversity. The Word of God that never fails is working mightily in me, causing my faith to be effective, in the Name of the Lord Jesus. I live a life of dominion and authority. Failure and defeat are not for me, in the Name of Jesus. I am strengthened in my inner-man and my resolve is solidified by the truth

MAJOR DAUGTER

of Your Word. I have my heart set on Your purpose for my life, and I refuse to be swayed by life's challenges, in Jesus' Name.

PROPHETIC PRAYER 7

I have life in its fullness; there is no death in my path. I can do all things through Christ who strengthens me. The joy of the Lord is my strength. Precious Lord, I thank You for Your Word of grace and power that builds me up and grants me my inheritance among the sanctified. As God's representative in this world, I decree peace and joy unspeakable in every area of my life, in the Name of Jesus. There are no accidents or mishaps on my path, for I walk in preordained pathways of blessings for me, today and always, in Jesus' Name. I walk in God's perfect will for my life today through the power of God's Word and by the working of God's Spirit, in Jesus' Name. I am born of God's Word and the Spirit of the Lord. Therefore, I am impregnable to everything that hurts or binds. Amen.

I thank You for Your Word of grace and power that builds me up and grants me my inheritance among the sanctified

PROPHETIC PRAYER 8

Precious Father, I thank You for Your goodness and the opportunity You have given me to bask in Your blessings and live the good life You have freely made available to me in Christ. Christ in me is the hope of my triumphant and glorious today, and my excellent and successful future because in Him I live, move and have my being; my life is secure in Him who causes all things to work together for my good! I live triumphantly by the Word today, excited that it is producing in me fruits unto

Christ in me is the hope of my triumphant and glorious today

righteousness, in Jesus' Name. I put my trust and confidence in Your Word, I am conscious that Your Word is all I need for progress, success and victory, in the Name of Jesus. Thank You for bringing me into a place of rest, progress, peace and victory, in the Name of Jesus. I refuse fear, worry, stress and doubt as I take advantage of the Lord's presence in and with me which leads, guides, protects and strengthens me. I am bold, strong and courageous, in the Name of Jesus. Thank You Lord, for Your glory that is revealed in me today, as I live conscious of Your power and presence, and I impact my world with Your glory, grace and righteousness, in Jesus' Name. I am led forth in victory and triumph today as the Word of God gains the mastery in my life, in Jesus' Name. Amen.

PROPHETIC PRAYER 9

Papa God, You are the strength of my life, and in You I have found success, divine rest, victory, joy, fulfilment and peace, in the Name of Jesus. The tests, trials and adversities that come my way are bread for me because I have been made more than a conqueror, and my faith is the victory that overcomes the world.

I am winning and reigning every day in life through the Spirit and by the Word of God

Glory to God! I am winning and reigning every day in life through the Spirit and by the Word of God! The Word of God is in my heart and in my mouth today, causing circumstances and situations to align with God's perfect will for my life, in the Name of Jesus. I reject every thought of worry and anxiety for I know that my faith in the mighty power of the Holy Spirit, and in God's Word, love and grace towards me is my victory over the devil and all the powers of darkness, in the Name of Jesus. I thank You for making my life pleasant and beautiful and for giving me a great future. I am forever grateful for the blood of Jesus that was shed; I have been purged of all unrighteousness and ushered into a life of perpetual victory. Now I have the God-life, peace in its fullness. I face each day with boldness and with full assurance that Christ is my advantage always; therefore, no matter the challenges that come my way, I am certain I will emerge victorious. God's grace puts me over and above in life! Hallelujah!

MAJOR DAUGTER

GO DEEPER

Romans 8:28; James 1:2-4; 1 Peter 5:7; 2 Corinthians 4:17; Proverbs 24:10; 1 John 4:4; 1 Corinthians 10:13; Psalm 127:2; Ecclesiastes 8:4

CHAPTER 7

SHORT DAILY PROPHETIC DECLARATIONS FOR PERSONAL STRENGTH AND WELL-BEING

MAJOR DAUGTER

"And in that day ye shall ask me nothing. Verily, verily, I say unto you, Whatsoever ye shall ask the Father in my Name, He will give it you. Hitherto have ye asked nothing in my Name: ask, and ye shall receive, that your joy may be full,"
John 16:23-24

There are many prayers offered with the closing remarks "through Jesus Christ, our Lord." However, when we look through Scripture, there is no place in which the Christian is asked to pray through any means or through Jesus. What the Bible teaches is that we pray in the Name of Jesus. This is the right way to pray. As a Christian, you do not need any kind of intermediary between you and the Father. Praying through Jesus is to make Him an intermediary between you

> *Praying through Jesus is to make Him an intermediary between you and the Father*

and the Father. Praying in the Name of Jesus means you are standing in the place of Jesus. As a Christian, Jesus has given you the legal right to use His Name. You have the right of attorney to function in His stead. This is the reason we cannot pray through Him. He has delegated His authority to you to use His Name as you desire. Jesus said, "I am the way, the truth and the life, no man cometh to the Father but by me" (John 14:6). In this verse, He was dealing with access. You gain this access by praying and asking in the Name of Jesus. When you have a need and you want to make a request to the Father, do it in the Name of Jesus. This is the sure way of having your request granted.

Remember, the Lord said "whatsoever." This means anything you desire. Wow! What an honour knowing that you can ask for whatever you want and receive it, when it is according to His will. His will is His Word. His Word states that you ask the Father, in the Name of Jesus. When you pray these prophetic prayers and make these declarations be bold and use the Name of Jesus.

Prophetic Declaration For A Job

I call for a job to manifest, in the Name of Jesus. I declare that my name is coming up; my CV is coming up for that job, for that opportunity, in the Name of Jesus. Gates of employment, whatever is holding you from real manifestation in my life, by the unchallengeable power of God, crash and open, in the Name of Jesus. Grace and anointing to get a job fall upon me, in Jesus' mighty Name. My Father, I plead the Blood of Jesus upon my job situation and ask for favour to come upon me during the interview, in the Name of Jesus. Amen. I claim the grace to overcome and to excel among all job competitors, in the Name of Jesus.

Grace and anointing to get a job fall upon me, in Jesus' mighty Name

Prophetic Declaration For A Salary Increase And Promotion

I decree and declare that the power of promotion is at work in me and in my life. Therefore, I am increasing in every area of my life. I am heaping success upon success, in Jesus' Name. I am rising

I experience only the upward and forward movement in my life

higher and higher every day in every area of my life. I experience only the upward and forward movement in my life.

Prophetic Declaration For Stagnation

My success and prosperity is appearing unto all man, in Jesus' Name

I decree and declare by the power of the Spirit that I am making progress and moving forward in my life. My success and prosperity is appearing unto all man, in Jesus' Name.

Prophetic Declaration For Releasing Monies Owed To You

I release all the monies that are owed to me, in the Name of Jesus. I declare that all those who owe me money will not have rest until they have paid me back all that is due to me, in Jesus' Name. My Father, let everyone who owes me pay back speedily in the Name of Jesus. My Father, I lift up those who are in debt to me to You. Bless them so that they can pay me, in the Name of Jesus.

> *I release all the monies that are owed to me, in the Name of Jesus*

Prophetic Declaration For Dreams And Goals

I see my greatness, my increase and my influence bursting forth on every side, in the Name of Jesus

My mind is open to receive new ideas. I refuse to see myself small in life, for the God I serve is the limit-breaker. I see my greatness, my increase and my influence bursting forth on every side, in the Name of Jesus.

Prophetic Declaration For Expansion

Father, thank You for Your anointing, which causes me to grow, expand and multiply in whatever I lay my hands to do. I take advantage of that anointing

I take advantage of that anointing in my life today, in my job, my business and my finances, in Jesus' Name

in my life today, in my job, my business and my finances, in Jesus' Name.

PROPHETIC PRAYER FOR PROTECTION 1

Father GOD, You are my refuge. I trust in You and I am safe! You rescue me from hidden traps, You shield me from deadly hazards. Your outstretched arms protect me, under them I am perfectly safe, Your arms fend off all harm. I fear nothing, not wild wolves in the night, not flying arrows in the day, not disease that prowls through the darkness, not disaster that erupts at high noon. Even though others succumb all around, drop like flies right and left, no harm will even graze me. I stand untouched. Yes, because GOD is my refuge, Evil cannot get close to me, harm cannot get through the door. He ordered His angels to guard me wherever I go. If I stumble, they will catch me; their job is to keep me from falling. I walk unharmed among lions and serpents, and kick them from the path. He gets me out of any trouble. He gives me the best of care. When vultures swoop and circle, ready to eat me alive, when bullies come towards me, all are defeated and fall flat on their faces.

Your outstretched arms protect me, under them I am perfectly safe, Your arms fend off all harm

PROPHETIC PRAYER FOR PROTECTION 2

With Him on my side, I am fearless, afraid of no one and nothing. When vandals ride down ready to eat me alive, those bullies fall flat on their faces. When besieged, I am as calm as a baby. When all hell breaks loose, I am collected and cool. I am asking GOD for one thing, only one thing: To live with Him in His house my whole life long. I will contemplate His beauty; I will study at His feet. That is the only quiet, secure place in a noisy world.

God holds me head and shoulders above all who try to pull me down

The perfect getaway, far from the buzz of traffic. God holds me head and shoulders above all who try to pull me down. I am headed for His place to offer anthems that will raise the roof! Already I am singing God-songs; I am making music to GOD. Point me down Your highway, GOD; direct me along a well-lit street; show my enemies whose side You are on. Do not throw me to the dogs, those liars who are out to get me, filling the air with their threats. I am sure now I will see God's goodness in the earth. Stay with GOD! Take heart. Do not quit. (Psalms 91 and 27, MSG)

Prophetic Prayer For Transport And Journeys

Father, I pray for all those travelling by buses, taxis, cars, planes, or whatever mode of transport they are using. I declare no weapon formed against them shall prosper, no plague shall come near them and no evil shall befall them. I release the Glory of God against accidents, mishaps,

I release the Glory of God against accidents, mishaps, misfortunes and disasters on the way

misfortunes and disasters on the way, I declare that in their way there is life, in their way there is no death, in Jesus' Name. I declare that these ones shall not form part of victims of satanic schemes on the road, in the air, in the water or wherever they are travelling, in Jesus' Name. The angels of God surround their mode of transport, the hand of God is upon each and every one of them, the presence of God is in that transport right now, in the Name of Jesus. Therefore, for them it is a pleasant journey, a smooth journey. Hallelujah.

Prophetic Declaration For Those Bound By Bad Habits

Father, in the Name of Jesus, I pray for men and women who are held by habits of drugs, tobacco, alcohol and lusts. I command the power of these habits broken over their lives, I command every demon of these habits to leave their bodies now and they be loosed from such forces. In Jesus' Name, I declare them free forever.

MAJOR DAUGTER

CHAPTER 8

PROPHETIC PRAYERS FOR MARRIAGE AND FAMILY

"The earnest (heartfelt, continued) prayer of a righteous man makes tremendous power available [dynamic in its working]."
James 5:16b (AMP)

As a young believer, you realise that once you prayed, you witnessed an instant result. As you mature, it may seem as though your prayers are being delayed. These are times where what is required is prevailing prayers.

Prevailing prayer is that which secures an answer. Merely saying prayers is not offering prevailing prayer. The prevalence of prayer does not depend so much on quantity,

Understand that prayer does not change God. God is benevolent and predisposed to doing good to us

but on quality. This kind of prayer weighs heavily on your heart.

Understand that prayer does not change God. God is benevolent and predisposed to doing good to us.

Prevailing prayer is not the one you say once and leave. The scripture above says the "continued" prayer of a righteous man. This means that there is continuation in prayer. It speaks of persistence and perseverance with patience. This is patience with hope that there will be an answer.

You can prevail in prayers for your soul. This is called the travail of soul. *"...for as soon as Zion travailed, she brought forth her children."* Paul said in Galatians 4:19 *"My little children, of whom I travail in birth again until Christ be formed in you."* This implies that he had travailed in birth for them before they were converted.

Be patient and full of hope, knowing there will be a change as you offer these prevailing prayers for marriage and family

Maybe you have been praying for a long time and it seems there is no change. Do not give up. In **James 5:17-18,** Elijah wanted to change the cause of nature. He prayed earnestly and there was a change. The same scripture lets us know that he was a man like us. There are many cases of men who prevailed in prayers and received extraordinary results. Jacob wrestled with the angel. Daniel prayed for twenty-one days. The list goes on.

MAJOR DAUGTER

Maybe you have been praying for a long time for your marriage and family and it seems there is no change. Please, do not give up. Be patient and full of hope, knowing there will be a change as you offer these prevailing prayers for marriage and family.

PROPHETIC PRAYER 1

My Father, I call for calm and peace in families that are collapsing and on the verge of divorce, I declare restoration in these families, I declare that love, unity, peace, joy and happiness reign in these families. The plan of the enemy concerning the families is vanquished and destroyed. No weapon formed against marriages shall prosper. I come against every anti-marriage spirit that seeks to divide families and bring divorce and separation, I declare their power broken over the lives of these families and marriages. The

The Lord binds the families and marriages together with chords of love that cannot be broken

mercy of God speaks for these marriages, the husbands love their wives and the wives respect and submit to their husbands, everywhere there is faithfulness and trust. The Lord binds the families and marriages together with chords of love that cannot be broken. The sweetness in marriages is restored, in the Name of Jesus.

PROPHETIC PRAYER 2

My Father, I pray specially for families and loved ones, that the will of the Father prospers in their lives, that they may walk the paths of righteousness; and that any plan or strategy of the adversary regarding them shall not prevail. I pray for families who are addicted to drugs, I stop the hand of Satan against them, in Jesus' Name. Any husband or wife who is tormented, I come against the power of Satan over their lives. I command the husbands and the wives to yield to the Holy Spirit. I declare that families that are not saved or born again yield to God. I stand against sudden danger. I stand against sudden death. From today in the area of marriage these families go out with joy and see joy for the rest of their lives. Instead of thorns they see fir trees in their marriages. Their marriages exalt the Name of the Lord. No weapon formed against these marriages shall prosper, in Jesus' Name.

> *I pray for families who are addicted to drugs, I stop the hand of Satan against them, in Jesus' Name*

PROPHETIC PRAYER 3

I declare that husbands and wives all over the world consider their promises to each other that were made in the presence of God who remembers their pledges and helps them by His Spirit in performing them. They are mindful of the fact that they are both the object of Christ's redemption and should neither be neglected nor belittled by the other. I decree and declare that they esteem each other as God's gift for mutual aid, comfort and joy, and as a repository of complete confidence and trust. They share willingly their joys and difficulties, successes and

They are mindful of the fact that they are both the object of Christ's redemption and should neither be neglected nor belittled by the other

challenges and they are neither conceited by the former, nor depressed by the latter. They cleave closely to each other in spirit and in truth. They meet difficulties with a united strength and victories with a united joy.

PROPHETIC PRAYER 4

Dear Father, I declare that their home is a place for couples and families to take refuge from the storms of life, not only for themselves but also for others who may be their guests. Father, may their home be a haven for the weary, a source of upliftment for the discouraged and a convincing testimony in a cynical world. May they recognise, therefore, the Lord Jesus Christ as the Head of their home, the Lord of their lives and the Personality of their deepest affection. Finally, as they do, Lord Jesus, confirm their marriage by Your guidance and let Your will overshadow their home with peace. May they love the Lord and serve Him with sincere hearts all the days of their lives, in Jesus' Name, Amen. Hallelujah!

May they love the Lord and serve Him with sincere hearts all the days of their lives, in Jesus' Name

PROPHETIC PRAYER 5

I decree and declare that husbands and wives are blessed in the city, and they are blessed in the field. The fruit of their body is blessed, and the fruit of their business and job is blessed and increased. They are blessed coming in and they are blessed going out. Everyone who declares himself or herself their enemy and anyone who rises against them is defeated before their face. Anyone who gathers against them gathers to scatter. They shall come against them in one way but

They are blessed coming in and they are blessed going out

they shall flee in seven ways. I speak increase upon every area of their lives. I decree and declare that they have a surplus of prosperity, through the fruit of their body, of their business, and of their jobs. They lend to many nations, and borrow from none. I decree that they are the head, and not the tail; and they live from above only. Life for them is upward and forward only. One way only, no reverse gear, hallelujah.

Prophetic Prayer For Love

Their words are seasoned with grace; they don't call each other names. Their words reflect God's nature. The anointing of the Holy Ghost is coming to their homes. It is taking away torments, tensions, arguments. Fights and anger are a thing of the past. They are not controlled by mood swings. They have the spirit of joy and praise, hallelujah. They spread joy, love, peace and happiness. They are a forcefield.

Prophetic Prayer For Fruit Of The Womb

Their wives are a fruitful vine; there is no barrenness in their lives. Those who have been struggling to conceive children, may they have a testimony, in Jesus' Name. There is a cry of babies. The Lord is turning many into mothers and fathers. They are fruitful; there's a multiplication in the families. They carry their children, in Jesus' Name. I stand on Exodus 23:26 In your land no woman will have a miscarriage or be without children. I will give you long lives. (GNT)

Prophetic Prayer For Pregnant Women

I pray for all pregnant women, all expectant mothers around the world. As I stand in the gap for them, I declare no complications with the pregnancy, in the Name of Jesus. Every woman expecting a child will carry the pregnancy to full term and every pregnancy will carry its full course. I come against every threat of miscarriage, I decree and declare that none shall cast their young before time, in Jesus' Name. I come against accidents. I come against mishandling of doctors, nurses and midwives, wrong prescriptions and all other bad interventions whatsoever. I release angels to guide and direct the doctors, nurses and midwives, in the Name of Jesus. No doctor will mislead them, no nurse will mislead them. I decree health for the mothers and health for the babies. I decree and declare that every child will be born healthy and strong and will be a blessing to every family, in Jesus' Name. As the Word declares in Psalms 127:3, "Children are a gift from the Lord; they are a real blessing." And Job 21:9-12 says, "God does

I declare no complications with the pregnancy, in the Name of Jesus

not bring disaster on their homes; they never have to live in terror. Yes, all their cattle breed and give birth without trouble. Their children run and play like lambs and dance to the music of harps and flutes." (GNT)

MAJOR DAUGTER

CHAPTER 9

PROPHETIC PRAYERS FOR CHILDREN, TEENAGERS AND YOUTH

PROPHETIC PRAYER 1

My Father, I pray for youths and teenagers around the world. I call for an outpouring of the Spirit upon this generation, that the Lord be revealed to them in a greater dimension than they've known; and that the light of God may dawn on those who have been prevented from the gospel in many nations; for there shall be a move of the Spirit across the world that shall sweep through heathen and antichrist cultures, and the harvest shall be great, saith the Lord.

> *My Father, I pray for youths and teenagers around the world.*

PROPHETIC PRAYER 2

My Father, I pray for children all over the world, that Your mighty hand of protection will rest upon them, guiding and shielding them from harm, evil and pestilence. I thank You, for Your wisdom granted them to recognise the path and the way of truth and righteousness, that they may grow thereby, in Jesus' Name. I pray specially for children around the world who are sick and suffering from different sicknesses, oh, that the healing power of Christ would touch them, relieving them of pain and bringing complete restoration. I pray for teenagers around the world, that

I pray for those who have not received Christ all around the world

they be guided continually in God's perfect will for their lives, and rescued from wicked and unreasonable men. I pray for those who have not received Christ all around the world, that they will receive the gospel and fulfil their purpose in Christ. I pray for school children who travel together in buses, that the wicked plans of Satan be frustrated. I declare that they are protected against accidents and mishaps on the road.

MAJOR DAUGTER

CHAPTER 10

PROPHETIC PRAYERS FOR CHRISTIANS AROUND THE WORLD

PROPHETIC PRAYER 1

My Father, I pray for God's people all around the world today, that they might be filled with the knowledge of God's will, in all wisdom and spiritual understanding, being fruitful in every good work, and increasing in the knowledge of God, in Jesus' Name. I pray for God's people who are challenged health-wise, I stop the hand of Satan upon their lives. I come against infirmities, I come against sudden danger, sudden death, I

I pray for God's people who are challenged health-wise, I stop the hand of Satan upon their lives

decree that in their way there's life, in their way there's victory. No weapon fashioned against them shall prosper they are protected on the left and on the right, even in the midst of the enemies, that which concerns them is perfected in their favour and what God has given them shall not be taken away from them, in Jesus' Name. No evil shall befall them; in Christ Jesus, they've overcome the world. I commit their plans, projects, jobs, business and everything that is of concern to them I commit it to God expecting God's intervention. I proclaim victory in their expectations. Any satanic force trying to frustrate them is paralysed.

The wisdom of God functions mightily in every one of God's children causing them to walk in the path of righteousness, the path that God preordained for them to walk in.

PROPHETIC PRAYER 2

I declare that the force of God's Spirit will continually pull divine opportunities towards God's people, jobs and businesses. They are waxing violently in the Spirit and the anointing of God is distinguishing them, they are increasingly stronger and making remarkable progress in all their endeavours. I

I declare a new level and a new season for God's people

declare that they are robustly nurtured with the rich teachings of the Word of God. I decree that they walk continually in the light of the Word of God in their finances, resulting in consistent and supernatural prosperity under God. I declare a new level and a new season for God's people. God's people are strengthened by His Spirit and by the Word. If there be anything that has weakened in their lives, it is strengthened now, in Jesus' Name. Everything negative is turned to their good and favour. Everything is turning around for their good, in Jesus' Name.

PROPHETIC PRAYER 3

I pray specifically against evil plots of the wicked against Christians around the world; that these evil schemes will fail, and the Lord's purpose for His people will prosper. I pray for Christians all around the world, that they may grow in grace and in the knowledge of our Lord and Saviour Jesus Christ, having the eyes of their spirits enlightened to comprehend the truth of God's Word, with the boldness to share the Word

I pray for Christians all over the world, that they be filled with the Spirit to preach the Word everywhere with boldness, that more souls may be saved

of God. I pray for Christians all over the world, that they be filled with the Spirit to preach the Word everywhere with boldness, that more souls may be saved. I Pray for deliverance of God's people from mass accidents and for safer mass travel around the world.

PROPHETIC PRAYER 4

I do not cease to give thanks for all Christians around the world. I pray that the God of our Lord Jesus Christ, the Father of glory, may give them the spirit of wisdom and revelation in the knowledge of Him. The eyes of their understanding being enlightened, that they may know the hope of His calling, the riches of the glory of His inheritance in the saints, and the exceeding greatness of His power toward us who believe, according to the working of His mighty power which He worked in Christ when He raised Him from the dead and seated Him at His right hand in the heavenly places, far above all principality and power and might and dominion, and every name that is named, not only in this age but also in that which is to come. He put all things under His feet, and gave Him to be head over all things to the church, which is His body, the fullness of Him who fills all in all.

I pray that the God of our Lord Jesus Christ, the Father of glory, may give them the spirit of wisdom and revelation in the knowledge of Him

PROPHETIC PRAYER 5

I pray for Christians around the world for their hearts not to fail by reason of evil and wickedness in the world, but to be strong and encouraged by the hope of the gospel as the only saving power of God in a world of darkness and turmoil. I pray for Christians undergoing severe persecution as a result of their faith in Christ, that they may be strengthened by God's Spirit in their hearts and that doors will be opened for freedom of

I pray for Christians to engage in soul-winning and evangelism activities more than ever, being conscious of the coming of our Lord Jesus Christ

expression of their faith. I pray for Christians who are ignorant of the truth and are held captive by false doctrines, that they will come in contact with the truth, thereby growing in knowledge unto the measure of the stature of the fullness of Christ. I pray for Christians to engage in soul-winning and evangelism activities more than ever, being conscious of the coming of our Lord Jesus Christ.

MAJOR DAUGTER

CHAPTER 11

PROPHETIC PRAYERS FOR MINISTERS OF THE GOSPEL AROUND THE WORLD

PROPHETIC PRAYER 1

Father, in the Name of Jesus, I pray for ministers of the gospel all around the world, I decree that their faith is strengthened and God's grace is granted to them to fulfil their calling, and they fulfil it without reproach. Hallelujah, they are protected from all evil, the hand of God is upon them mightily. I declare that the power of their voice is given to them and that they preach and teach the Word with boldness. I declare that they are delivered from unreasonable and wicked men, in Jesus' Name. I pray for ministers of the gospel who are facing challenges in their health and severe persecution in their churches.

I declare that they are delivered from unreasonable and wicked men, in Jesus' Name

I declare that things are turning around in their churches for their favour, I declare that the mercy of God and the kindness of God and the grace of God is extended to them for a restoration of their health and I command a speedy recovery for them in their health.

PROPHETIC PRAYER 2

I decree and declare that all ministers of God are lifted by the Spirit of God that the Spirit of God is giving them ideas that are moving them from one level to another. No evil shall befall them; the anointing of God rests upon them. I command all their dreams and plans to materialise speedily. I command every delay in their

They are above in all situations, not beneath, for the Word says they are the head and not the tail

expectations to be cut off, no more delay, angels are activated, things happen on their behalf, in Jesus' Name. They are above in all situations, not beneath, for the Word says they are the head and not the tail. I pray for ministers of the gospel in war-torn regions of the world that the Lord would deliver and protect them from unreasonable and wicked men, that the Word of the Lord may have free course and be glorified. I pray for the churches of Christ and their leaders across the world that He would grant them, according to the riches of His glory, to be strengthened with might by His Spirit in the inner man and filled with the comfort of the Spirit and hope and courage of the Word.

PROPHETIC PRAYER 3

I declare that ministers of the gospel around the world will continue to express boldness, preaching the gospel and demonstrating the power of God, with signs, wonders and miracles accompanying them everywhere. I cancel obnoxious laws offensive to Christianity and declare that venues for worship and preaching of the gospel are open and accessible for use.

I cancel obnoxious laws offensive to Christianity and declare that venues for worship and preaching of the gospel are open and accessible for use

CHAPTER 12

PROPHETIC PRAYERS FOR YOUR COUNTRY

Prayer is a ministry. It is not only to ask God for something, it is more than that. It is our responsibility to pray for others and the countries in which we live. When we stop doing so the Bible says we are sinning. "As for me, the Lord forbid that I should sin against Him by no longer praying for you. Instead, I will teach you what is good and right for you to do" (1 Samuel 12:23). We need to

> *"As for me, the Lord forbid that I should sin against Him by no longer praying for you. Instead, I will teach you what is good and right for you to do" (1 Samuel 12:23)*

understand that our prayers will affect the necessary changes that are needed in our countries. We should never give up the responsibility of prayer no matter what.

Isaiah 43:26 "Put me in remembrance let us plead together: declare thou, that thou mayest be justified."

This is a special invitation to prayer from God, our Father, because prayer is a caucus rendezvous between us and God. God calls us to present our cases before Him.

Let's break it down further.

"I exhort, therefore, that, first of all, supplications, prayers, intercessions, and giving of thanks be made for all men; for kings, and for all that are in authority; that we may lead a quiet and peaceable life in all godliness and honesty. For this is good and acceptable in the sight of God our Saviour; Who will have all men to be saved, and to come unto the knowledge of the truth."
1 Timothy 2:1-4

Reading the scripture above makes me really think. If we could take the Word of God as it is and become it, it would make a huge difference. Here, the scripture admonishes us that first of all, first things first, prayers should be made for others not ourselves. This means that, in prayer, we should not put ourselves first but others, and in the order that the scripture gives. I have observed that many times we tend to put ourselves first in prayer and in everything. Then, if things don't go well in our country or in our lives, we will ask God, why? Or even worse, blaming Him for everything. You will hear people say things such as, "Where was God? Why did He let it happen?"

MAJOR DAUGTER

We need to follow the right order. In the scripture above, the Word advises us that first we should pray for kings and all those in authority, not ourselves first and our families first; it is the other way around.

When the scripture says for kings and for all those in authority, it means that we are expected to pray for our government and all those who are in government, from the national, provincial and down to local levels. In those days, most countries had kings, but today the king is equivalent to our president. Then, for all that are in authority (verse 3) means we are expected to pray for all our leaders, the members of parliament, the ministers, the premiers, the

God's final purpose is for the gospel to spread. And this will happen when we have a good and peaceful government

mayors, the councillors, the union leaders, the policemen, the defence force, etc. Some of us may be doing this already but not enough of us. If we could take praying for our leaders seriously, then things would not be as they are in our country. This is a call to all of us to pray for our country and the leaders instead of criticising them.

The scripture above says we ought to pray for them so that we may lead a peaceable life. We need to understand that God cares about us affectionately and jealously so when we pray for those in authority, even if they are not Christians, God will answer our prayers and do what we ask Him to do for us, so that we may once again lead a peaceful and quiet life. What an honour and privilege we have with Our Father. Verse 3 says for this is good and acceptable in the sight of God our Saviour.

This means as Christians, if we do this and put first things first, we will please Our Father who will have all men to be saved, and to come to the knowledge of the truth. God's final purpose is for the gospel to spread. And this will happen when we have a good and peaceful government. That is why God wants us to pray for those in authority.

We need to stand in the gap for our beloved country and make a hedge as in Ezekiel 22:30-31. "And I sought for a man among them, that should make up the hedge, and stand in the gap before me for the land, that I should not destroy it: but I found none. Therefore have I poured out mine indignation upon them; I have consumed them with the fire of my wrath: their own way have I recompensed upon their heads, saith the Lord God."

In this scripture, God was looking for one person, one person only, who would pray and stand in the gap, and He would not destroy the land. So just one person could have saved the country. Today, God is looking for you to stand and pray on behalf of your country and make that hedge. The big Question is: are you available and willing to do that? God's intervention will only come when we as Christians seek His face and ask Him to move. That is it! So come on, ride with me.

PROPHETIC PRAYER 1

Father, in the Name of Jesus, we are praying for all those who live in South Africa (please put the name of your country here). We declare that the angels of God surround this country, the anointing of God is upon this country, peace is within the walls of this country, prosperity is within the walls of this country. We are praying for our Beloved Country South Africa (please put the name of your country here), for all those in authority, the president, the members of parliament, those in the

We pray that we will all live a quiet and peaceable life in all godliness

legislature, the judiciary, the ministers, the premiers, the mayors, the councillors, the union leaders, the leaders of student organisations, the leaders of youth organisations, the heads of parastatals, the leaders of political parties. We pray that we will all live a quiet and peaceable life in all godliness. We are praying for collaboration, mutual trust and understanding between the legislature, judiciary and executives, and all those in government, all those in different sectors, all those in positions of authority in the country and all our political parties.

PROPHETIC PRAYER 2

Papa God, I pray for peace to continue to reign in my country, that if there be any trouble brewing anywhere, it will not stand. I pray for right people to be in positions of authority, whose advisers are godly men. I come against corruption and pray that men in great positions will give their lives to Christ. I

I pray for right people to be in positions of authority, whose advisers are godly men

stop the violence and the wickedness in the country. That wicked spirit of evil, that principality of evil that has dominated the political realm of this country, I command you now, in the Name of Jesus, to get out of this realm. In the Name of Jesus, I reassign angels of God to take over this realm. I declare that peace continues to reign in my country and that there be stability and development in the economy and every sector. I pray for the prosperity, peace and stability of this country.

PROPHETIC PRAYER 3

I pray for those who are travelling by bus or train or plane against the plans of Satan to destroy lives. I declare that God's grace and mercy covers and delivers these commuters from the destruction of Satan. I declare that accidents, mishaps and disasters are minimised in my country. I come against violence, corruption and greed, that

I declare that God's grace and mercy covers and delivers these commuters from the destruction of Satan

such will be dismantled completely through my prayers. I pray against those who yield themselves to satanic influences to execute evil, protests, wars, raids with the intention to destroy lives and property. I decree that their plans be brought to nought. They will conjure powers and those powers will fail. I pray for Christians in this country, that they are protected from harm; their steps are ordered by the Lord. The peace of God guards their hearts. The light of the gospel shines and prevails in this country over every law, policy, constitution or custom.

MAJOR DAUGTER

CHAPTER 13

PROPHETIC PRAYERS FOR COUNTRIES OF THE WORLD

MAJOR DAUGTER

"I exhort therefore, that, first of all, supplications, prayers, intercessions, and giving of thanks, be made for all men."
1 Timothy 2:1

Prayer is the most potent force known to humanity. We have been ordained to receive answers to prayers. However, as Christians, we must not be selfish in our prayers. Prayer is a weapon that can be used to change anything and thwarts the wits of the adversary. This kind of weaponry is something God invites us to use as we seek not only our personal transformation, but that of others and the world at large. We have been called into the ministry of intercession.

An intercessor is one who takes up a burden that goes far beyond his or her personal needs. We have the authority as Christians to pray for others, pushing back the darkness of sin and oppression on their lives. Intercession is prayer that pleads with God for your needs and especially those of others. The ministry of intercession is what will hold God to His promises regarding our lives. This could be personal, family, a city or even a whole nation.

Intercession is warfare. It is the key to God's battle plan for our lives. In as much as we know it is a battle, it is not physical, but spiritual. Intercessory prayer is also prayer that does not give up. It is the kind of prayer that endures all setbacks and overcomes every obstacle. It is the kind that presses on until God's will concerning the situation (Philippians 3:12).

Your intercession can move the hand of God. He is anxious to answer your prayers. There are many benefits of being an intercessor. Intercession enhances our own spiritual growth. Praying for others causes us to become more like Christ, who spent many hours praying to His Father for others. You cannot pray for change in the lives of

Your intercession can move the hand of God. He is anxious to answer your prayers

people, without experiencing positive change yourself. Your relationship with God gets closer every time you pray for someone else.

MAJOR DAUGTER

When we intercede, it helps us to focus on someone other than ourselves. It helps us to be selfless, just like Jesus. There is so much joy to be experienced each time you see the result of the prayers in the lives of the people you pray for. Rise to this call and see your life transcend from glory to glory as you pray for countries of the world.

PROPHETIC PRAYER 1

I pray for peace around the world. I pray for the spread of the gospel around the world, that many more would come to the knowledge of the Truth, and the Name of Jesus Christ be glorified. I pray for those suffering from sickness and disease, wounds and injuries around the world in war-torn regions that through the grace of Christ, healing will result for them quickly. I pray for men, women and children who are held against their will, abused,

I pray for those suffering from sickness and disease, wounds and injuries around the world

tortured and exploited in secret camps and horror homes around the world; that the grace of Christ be extended to them, and the Lord intervene in their situation and deliver them from the dark forces of wickedness holding them in satanic isolation; that they be restored and enabled to live a normal life. I pray for those who are being persecuted around the world, I pray against the growing hostility to the Church of Christ in some nations of the world, that the gospel of Christ may prevail in these countries, and many be turned to the Lord. I pray for the increased ministry of the gospel around the world, and I pray specially for political leaders who are Christians, that the Lord Jesus Christ may remain the central focus of their deepest interests, in Jesus' Name.

PROPHETIC PRAYER 2

I pray for the political leaders of countries of the world, that those who have never known Christ may hear and receive the Word of salvation, for the time is short and the Lord is coming back again. I pray for refugees all over the world, I pray for their well-being, protection, preservation and realisation of their hopes and aspirations for a better life, and that even in their difficult positions, may they still accept and embrace the gospel. My Father, I recognise the special place Jerusalem holds in the prophetic revelation in Your Word. I pray for the peace of

Christ may hear and receive the Word of salvation, for the time is short and the Lord is coming back again

Jerusalem and that the gospel of Christ may have free course in all Israel and be glorified. I pray for leaders of countries, that they may be guided by the Lord to make the right decisions and use the powers of state for the benefit, progress, security and peace of their people. I come against extreme weather conditions around the world; that as the Lord Jesus calmed the storms, may these conditions be calmed for Christians' sake and the gospel's, with miracle deliverances for many. I

MAJOR DAUGTER

stand in the gap for the nations, for the forgiveness of sins and salvation of souls in these nations.

PROPHETIC PRAYER 3

I stand in the gap for world leaders as they steer the ships of their countries and for all in positions of authority; that we may live peaceful and progressive lives in all godliness and reverence; and for the increased influence of the gospel in all nations leading to the salvation of many. Jesus said: "And there shall be upon the earth distress of countries with perplexity ... Men's hearts failing them for fear, and for looking after those things which are

I pray for the peace and healing of the countries and for their economies, as many are in distress and perplexed, as Jesus prophesied

coming on the earth" (Luke 21:26). I pray for the peace and healing of the countries and for their economies, as many are in distress and perplexed, as Jesus prophesied. Oh! That the Word of the Lord may have free course and be glorified.

Prophetic Prayers For Laws And Policies

I pray for countries under bondage of obnoxious laws, I break the powers of such laws and their satanic influences, I declare that the gospel is gaining entrance into the corridors of power and righteousness will be exalted in these countries.

Prophetic Prayer For The Economy

I pray for countries who are under severe economic hardship, that those in authority would embrace the wisdom of God to rule and guide the affairs of their countries as they yield themselves to the Spirit of God.

Prophetic Prayer For Natural Disasters

I pray for countries experiencing natural disasters which claim lives and properties. I release and direct the power of God to put an end to all such evil.

Prophetic Prayer Against Terrorism

I pray for protection of God's people against terrorist attacks in the cities and countries of the world, I cancel such evil plots against people and I declare that the power of God subdues and overthrows such evil in the hearts and minds of these plotters, disabling their abilities and attempts, in Jesus' Name.

MAJOR DAUGTER

CHAPTER 14

PROPHETIC DECLARATIONS OVER BAD AND SATANIC DREAMS

CALL TO ACTION

You must learn how to cream your dream. It is of no significant how horrific the dream is. You can cream and give it the interpretation you want. Refuse to fret about bad dreams. You can use prayer to stop scatter, reassign or totally cream the dream to favour you. Instead of panicking, go on your knees in prayers to deal with it. Pray like this when you dreamt of what you do not like.

Father in the matchless Name of Jesus Christ, I scatter every negative effects of this dream. I declare it shall have no impact in my life or in my destiny. Lord, as You declare in Your Word, that "...It shall not stand, and it shall not come to pass." So I affirm that no negative dream shall come to pass in my life. Amen.

PROPHETIC DECLARATION 1

I declare by the power of the Holy Spirit that my sleeps are characterize with sweet dreams. In the mighty Name of Jesus Christ, I refuse nightmares in my dreams. My dreams are revelations from the Lord to me. They have Holy Spirit inspired meaning and directions. Halleluiah!

I accept only the good things from my dreams, in Jesus' Name. Every evil through dreams that the devil tries to use to manipulate my life, I cancel by fire! Anything orchestrated by the devil to interfere with my dreams or to cause me to fear through dreams, I consume it with the fire of the Holy Ghost. Every

I accept only the good things from my dreams, in Jesus' Name

manipulation through dreams, I rebuke in the precious Name of Jesus Christ. Every dream that I have dreamt in the past that the devil is using to attack my life and destiny, receive fire! Every dream that originates from the coven or the pit of hell to cause me to mourn, receive brimstone and thunder, in Jesus' Name. Every act of wickedness set against my life, I scatter by thunderous fire, in Jesus' Name.

157

PROPHETIC DECLARATION 2

By the power of the Holy Spirit at work in me, I declare that I can cream my dreams to what I want them to be. It is the interpretation and meaning I give to my dream, that is what they become in the Name of Jesus Christ.

I declare that all the negative dreams I ever had and that I will ever dream are converted to positive and impactful meaning in the Name of Jesus Christ

Therefore, I declare that all the negative dreams I ever had and that I will ever dream are converted to positive and impactful meaning in the Name of Jesus Christ. Every dream of death, receive life interpretation and meaning, in Jesus' Name. Dreams of stagnation, backwardness, losses and bitterness, I convert your meanings and impacts to blessings and fruitfulness, in Jesus' Name.

In the Name of Jesus Christ, I cream every failure from my dreams to success; every defeat to success; every curse to blessing and every poverty to prosperity. I cream every loss to gain; every defeat to victory and every sickness to divine health, in Jesus Name. Amen.

158

In the Name of Jesus Christ of Nazareth, I refuse to have anything to do with the marine world. I declare that I do not have any marine world family, business, finances or bank accounts. I will only have a spouse, children, businesses, and money and bank details by natural processes in Jesus Name. Anything connecting me to the negative supernatural, receive thunderous fire from heaven in Jesus' Name. I cancel all evil and satanic dreams and their impact in my life by fire. I call forth fire seven times upon all gatherings against me, my family and all that concerns me.

PROPHETIC PRAYER

Father in the Name of Jesus Christ, I uproot every seed of sickness, barrenness, and wastefulness planted by the enemy in my dreams by fire! I call fire upon every work of witches and wizard through my dreams in the Name of Jesus Christ. Every snare of the fowler in forms of spiritual arrows and bullets against my life, family, and business fall down by the rain of fire.

You spirits sent to monitor my life and progress die, die, die by earthquakes in Jesus' Name. I break to pieces every spirit daggers and spears attacking my marriage, in the Name of Jesus Christ. I drown to death every marine spirit the devil is using to disturb my marriage and family. I discomfit the camp of the enemy by brimstone and fire.

My dreams are opportunity for revelations and instructions from God. Therefore, every dream manipulator die, die, die, die! I disband every negative orchestrations by the devil and his cohorts through dreams, in Jesus Name. Amen. I cream every dream of darkness and command it to receive light by the power of the Holy Spirit. Every dream, vision, word, thought and contemplation working against my progress and advancement in life, receive the fire of Prophet Elijah, in Jesus' Name. Amen.

MAJOR DAUGTER

CHAPTER 15

NOT FOR BABES

MAJOR DAUGTER

This section is for the spiritually matured who can handle dangerous spiritual warfare attacks and can counter-attack the enemies to flee. So if you are not bold or spiritually fortified enough, beware! The Word of God says, *"Everyone who lives on milk is still an infant, inexperienced in the message of righteousness. But solid food is for the mature, the ones by constant use having trained the senses for distinguishing both good and evil"* Hebrews 5: 13 – 14.

The spiritually immature are the infants who still live on the elementary – milk. The spiritually matured and fortified are the ones that are trained and experienced in dealing with wicked spiritual forces. They are the ones this section is meant for.

Declarations To Revoke Financial Liability

"If you fully obey the Lord your God and carefully keep all his commands that I am giving you today, the Lord your God will set you high above all the nations of the world. You will experience all these blessings if you obey the Lord your God: Your towns and your fields will be blessed. Your children and your crops will be blessed. The offspring of your herds and flocks will be blessed. Your fruit baskets and breadboards will be blessed. Wherever you go and whatever you do, you will be blessed. "The Lord will conquer your enemies when they attack you. They will attack you from one direction, but they will scatter from you in seven! "The Lord will guarantee a blessing on everything you do and will fill your storehouses with grain. The Lord your God will bless you in the land he is giving you. "If you obey the commands of the Lord your God and walk in his ways, the Lord will establish you as his holy people as he swore he would do. Then all the nations of the world will see that you are a people claimed by the Lord, and they will stand in awe of you. "The Lord will give you prosperity in the land he swore to your ancestors to give you, blessing you with many children, numerous livestock, and abundant crops. The Lord will send rain at the proper time from his rich

treasury in the heavens and will bless all the work you do. You will lend to many nations, but you will never need to borrow from them. If you listen to these commands of the Lord your God that I am giving you today, and if you carefully obey them, the Lord will make you the head and not the tail, and you will always be on top and never at the bottom"

Deuteronomy 28: 1 – 13

PROPHETIC DECLARATION 1

The Word of God says it is my portion to lend to others and not to be in debt. Therefore, I proclaim by the power of the Holy Spirit that debt is not my portion, in the Name of the Lord Jesus Christ.

All that the caterpillars and cankerworms have eaten that belong to me; all that belong to me in the camp of the enemy, I retrieve them, in the mighty Name of Jesus Christ.

I declare that I am above only; I cannot be drowned in any form of financial crisis, by the power of the Holy Spirit.

I affirm in the Name of Jesus Christ that my finances are secured and protected from the devourer.

You wicked spirits that burn up my money; you forces that devalues my money, I rebuke you and I command the restoration of all my money by fire.

I rebuke you forces that tear my cheque books in my dreams. You wicked demons that put holes in my pockets in my dreams fall down and die by fire.

MAJOR DAUGTER

I declare that my wasted years, energies and resources be restored back to me now, in Jesus' Name.

PROPHETIC DECLARATION 2

You monitoring spirits monitoring and stealing my blessings, wherever you are from suffocate and die, in Jesus Name. Amen.

O' South Africa, you are free from your spoilers. Your adversaries that steal your common patrimonies are judged with fire and brimstone, in Jesus' Name.

O' South Africa, the enemies that divert your affluence; that cause poverty in your land are consumed by thunder strikes and fire, in Jesus' Name.

I divert all darts of the devil and his cohorts send after my business, finances and resources, receive fire and die, in Jesus' Name.

I rebuke every devil that aborts miracles and blessings, I render your power useless, in the Name of Jesus Christ.

PROPHETIC DECLARATION 3

Father, You alone are Worthy and there is none like You. All other gods are sinking sand.

In the Name of Jesus Christ, I cast out every spirit that secretly leaks information about my progress and blessings, receive fire, fire, fire, fire.

Anywhere the evil ones are gathered against me, I command fire to fall on them. Every flying spirit being used against me receives thunder and brimstone, in Jesus' Name.

Every manipulation of the enemy anchored to my life, receive Holy Ghost fire, in the Name of Jesus Christ.

I declare that my name is mentioned for good and favor. The Name of the Lord Jesus Christ is named upon my life. Amen.

I declare that I have a great day every day of my life. My joy, peace, prosperity, will not be stolen by the enemies, in Jesus' Name.

I declare that everywhere I turn, goodness shall locate me; from the North, South, East and West, I receive blessings, in Jesus' Name.

My life is filled with God's goodness, greatness, kindness, fruitfulness, and all that I ever desire of the Lord, in Jesus' Name.

Resuscitating Prayers For Those Given Few Days To Live

Pray this prayer before going to bed every night.

Father Lord God, You are my shield, strong and breasted One. In You I live, move and have my being. Lord Jesus, by the power in Your Name, I declare that no weapon of the enemy formed against me shall prevail. I have a prevailing spiritual arsenal to destroy all plans and manipulations of the devil.

Affirm that I will not die and that Jesus Christ is my life. He is the Lord of my spirit, soul and flesh. In the Name of Jesus Christ, I release ballistic missiles of fire and thunder into the camp of the enemy.

I have passed from death to life. The Holy Spirit vitalizes my mortal body. Every fiber of my being is inundated with eternal life, in Jesus' Name. Amen.

Affirm These As Many Times As Possible Daily

In the Name of Jesus Christ of Nazareth, I affirm that my body is the temple of the Holy Spirit. Thus, sicknesses, diseases, afflictions and pains cannot coexist with the Holy Spirit in my body.

I affirm that there is no death in my path. I have no path with hell or anything hatched out of it, in Jesus' Name. Amen.

I declare that the shadow of death hovering around me is destroyed by fire, in the mighty Name of Jesus Christ.

I declare that every fiber of my being, cell of my blood and organs of my body have life in them. They function optimally in their right quality and quantity in the Name of Jesus Christ. Amen.

I declare that I receive the power and grace of resurrection, it flows in me mightily causing me to be healed of every sickness and infirmities that have bedridden me, In the Name of Jesus Christ. Amen.

PRAY THESE PRAYERS DAILY

O' You Voice that calms the raging sea, speak to my body and situation now, in Jesus' Name.

O' You Voice of resurrection, You spoke to the widow's Son and he came back to life; You called forth Lazarus from the grave and he heard You. Today, I ask that You speak also to my circumstances now by fire.

O' You Voice that can calm the storm, raise the dead, command fish, speak to unstop ears and command trees to die. Speak to me and change my situation, in the Name of Jesus Christ. Amen.

I declare that all the forces pursuing me with coffins fall down and die by fire. You are the ones the coffins are meant for, in Jesus Name. Amen.

I soak myself in the blood of Jesus Christ. It washes away every sin and sickness in my life in the Name of Jesus Christ.

O' resurrecting power of the Holy Spirit, lift me out of this dungeon of sickness by fire. Amen.

Prophetic Declaration For House/Vehicle Repossession/Court Cases

"Instead of your shame you shall have double honor, and instead of confusion they shall rejoice in their portion. Therefore in their land they shall possess double; Everlasting joy shall be theirs."

Isaiah 61:7

MAJOR DAUGTER

PROPHETIC DECLARATION FOR ACQUITTAL 1

O' God my Father, look down from heaven upon the evil conspiracies against me. O' Lord, overturn every decision made against me with your holy fire from heaven, in Jesus' Name.

Every plan and decision of the enemy to bring shame upon my life, receive fire. I destroy you spirits of shame set out to embarrass me, in Jesus' Name.

I void evil ordinances made against me. All constructs and manipulations to imprison me physically and spiritually, receive the judgment of God by fire, in Jesus' Name.

You wicked gathering seeking to pull me down by all means, I shoot you down by thunder. Every consultation made with the intension to work against me, I rebuke you, in Jesus' Name.

Every plan to stall my blessings or to postpone my benefits, I taut life out of those plans by fire, in Jesus' Name.

Every court sitting against me both in the physical and in the spiritual realms, receive seven gun shots and die, in Jesus' Name.

PROPHETIC DECLARATION FOR ACQUITTAL 2

The Judgment of God is against every lawsuit perpetuated against me. I receive the acquittal of heaven against every evil documents filed against me, in Jesus' Name.

I seize the power of the earth to entertain or to acknowledge any case against me by fire and brimstone, in the Name of Jesus Christ.

I call down fire from heaven to fall upon and dissolve every orchestration of the enemy by fire, in Jesus' Name.

In the Name of Jesus Christ, every signal, and correspondence between the spiritual and the physical realms designed to work against me, I frustrate your efforts. Receive fire and thunder.

PROPHETIC DECLARATION FOR ACQUITTAL 3

Every conspiracy designed to frustrate my life, I frustrate your efforts too, in Jesus' Name. You shall not succeed in your enterprise, in Jesus' Name.

I rain fire and brimstone upon every physical and spiritual place the evil ones are meeting to plan my downfall. Every means of communication and transportation that they use, receive fire, in Jesus' Name.

I declare that the wickedness of my enemies will be compounded against them. Their acts of witchcraft return to frustrate them in the Name of Jesus Christ.

I exalt the horns of those who are mindful of my progress and advancement. Promotion and blessing are theirs in Jesus' Name. They will never know lack or dryness, in Jesus' Mighty Name.

All those who seek my fall, disgrace and defeat are yours. Those who scheme for my downfall, you shall carry with your heads your plans, in Jesus' Name.

MAJOR DAUGTER

I send arrows by thunder into the camp of the enemy.
They shall eat the fruits of their wickedness.

PROPHETIC DECLARATION FOR ACQUITTAL 4

They will be stripped by the stones of disgrace and defeat. Their mistakes will consume them in the Name of Jesus Christ.

In the Name of Jesus Christ of Nazareth, every familiar spirit monitoring my life, cease on your tracks by fire. You spirits and forces of hell that plan to disrupt my life with sickness, pains, and all your wicked acts, receive thunderous fire and brimstone.

O' God of heaven, fight my course. Be strong on my behalf. Let my enemies know that I am serving a living God, in Jesus Name.

Every gang up of my adversaries to implicate me, receive fire; every documentation presented to incriminate me catch fire. And every manipulation of my files to stagnate my promotion receive seven shots of arrows, in Jesus' Name.

I declare that the mountains and hills will burst into songs, and the trees of the field will clap their hands as I testify of the goodness of God in my life. Yes, nations shall come to my light and kings to the brightness of

MAJOR DAUGTER

my rising because the Lord has done marvellous
things in my life.

CONCLUSION

"Words are important. Wherever you are now or where you want to be shall be determined by your words. For by thy words thou shalt be justified, and by thy words thou shalt be condemned."
Matthew 12:37

"Being born again, not of corruptible seed, but of incorruptible, by the Word of God, which liveth and abideth for ever."
1 Peter 1:23

Say what God has said in consent to His Word. Every living thing must remain connected to its source for its continued existence. You can only be sustained by the continued connection to your source.
Genesis 1:9-16, 20-28; 2:7

MAJOR DAUGTER

Your physical life came from the ground. Your spirit being came from the Word of God. Our life originates from God. The life we have has gone past the life from the Word. The life we have now is the life of the Word. God's Word is powerful and never fails in what it intends to accomplish.

So shall my Word be that goeth forth out of my mouth: it shall not return unto Me void, but it shall accomplish that which I please, and it shall prosper in the thing whereto I sent it. Isaiah 55:11

Words are vehicles; they transport faith or fear, love or hate, life or death. Ask yourself what do your words transport when you speak? Or what have you been transporting?

Matthew 12:36 "But I say unto you, that every idle word that men shall speak, they shall give account thereof in the day of judgement."

Words are seeds, and they produce after their kind; they produce what they say.

Luke 8:11 "Now the parable is this: The seed is the Word of God."

Words are amplifiers. They amplify the thoughts of your heart, and they reveal your character.

Luke 4:36, 37 "And they were all amazed, and spake among themselves, saying, 'What a Word is this! For with authority and power He commandeth the unclean spirits, and they come out.' And the fame of Him went out into every place of the country round about."

It is important HOW you use your words.

Agreeing with the Word and confessing the Word are two different things. Most people agree with the Word but don't confess it. It is when you confess the Word that it makes a difference in your situation. The Word must be spoken to produce results as seed must be sown to have a crop/harvest. Agreeing with the Word just means you have seed, but that doesn't mean the seed is sown. Until the seed is sown, you're not going to have a crop/harvest.

MAJOR DAUGTER

GO DEEPER

Genesis 17:1-6; Hebrews 4:12; 12:17; 13:5-6; Psalm
107:17-20; 119:89-90; John 6:63; 15:7

If this book has been a blessing to you, please share your testimony with the whole world by sending us an email to:

majorwnl@majordaughterlive.com

JOIN OUR DIGITAL COMMUNITY

FACEBOOK: Major Daughter Live

TWITTER: @major_daughter

MAJOR DAUGTER

www.ingramcontent.com/pod-product-compliance
Lightning Source LLC
LaVergne TN
LVHW041316080426
835513LV00008B/489